Meditation Now:
A Beginner's Guide

D0802189

A BEGINNER'S GUIDE

Meditation Now

10-Minute Meditations to Restore Calm and Joy, Anytime, Anywhere

ELIZABETH RENINGER

ALTHEA
PRESS

Before You Begin

Yes, meditation is for you.
The benefits of meditation are available to everyone—regardless of age, health, gender, race, religious affiliation (or lack thereof), or level of education. All that's required is genuine interest.

Everything you need is already within you.
Meditation doesn't require any extra equipment. Your precious human body-mind is both the territory you'll be exploring as well as the observational tool you will be using.

All are welcome.
Meditation is not about rejecting thoughts, emotions, or any other aspect of experience. Instead, you'll learn how to give these phenomena lots of space rather than getting wrapped up in them.

Live the experience instead of thinking it.
Like the taste of a peach, the fruits of meditation are experiential: truly known only by you. The guidance here is offered like a peach in the hand of a friend: yours now to accept, taste, and enjoy.

Have fun!
Try to think of the meditation practices as play more than work. Trust that there is much of value to discover, and take a childlike approach—be endlessly curious and open to the adventure.

CONTENTS

INTRODUCTION

Welcome! This book is for those of you who are brand new to meditation. It's also for those who have tried meditation and are now ready to revisit the basics and perhaps establish a more consistent practice. Within its pages, you'll find a variety of exercises easily incorporated—as ten-minute breaks—into your busy day. They'll help you reconnect with the peace and joy that is your natural state.

The term "meditation" refers to practices for training the mind and tuning into the aware presence that is the background of all of life's experiences. It can involve a wide variety of techniques designed to promote relaxation, enhance energy, improve concentration, and develop compassion. The most general purpose of meditation is to cultivate an abiding sense of well-being throughout life's activities. In this book, through a series of user-friendly exercises and discussions, you'll be introduced to the core principles of this ancient practice. You'll learn the art and science of silent introspection—of giving your body and mind a rest, while remaining fully awake and observant.

There's a great bumper sticker (perhaps you've seen it) that reads: "Don't believe everything you think." This good advice points to an insight that is cultivated through meditation: You don't have to respond to that chattering voice in your mind, that never-ending stream of thoughts. You don't have to get caught up in the whirlwind of its dramas. Instead, you can learn to observe the thoughts in your mind in a similar way to how you might watch a movie.

Knowing you are separate from what is happening on the big screen allows you to enjoy the film. Likewise, taking a stand as the witness (the observer of your thoughts) helps you retain your independence—your freedom—from the "movie" playing in your mind. You can also think of yourself as an actor: A skilled Shakespearean actor playing Hamlet on stage recites his lines with passion and precision—without for a moment believing he is, in reality, Hamlet. Similarly, you can allow the various dialogues to unfold in your mind without believing you are your thoughts or even that they are true. To see this clearly is one of the fruits of meditation.

Through the simple exercises presented in this book, you will:

- Learn how to calm and befriend that internal chatter in your mind that so frequently seems to operate on autopilot.

- Be introduced to 32 unique meditations that can be practiced, in ten-minute periods, anytime, anywhere—for an abundance of choice and flexibility.

- Receive tips for applying meditation at work and on the go, as well as allowing mindfulness to naturally be part of your daily activities, such as eating, driving, and taking care of household chores.

- Learn about common obstacles to successful meditation and how to overcome them.

- Be guided through Loving-Kindness and Appreciation meditations to generate positive energy, and explore productive ways of relating to difficult thoughts and feelings.

- Have access to three 28-day programs; structured guidance to support your practice.

PART ONE

Beginning Your Journey

_____

Meditation is not a way of making your mind quiet.
It is a way of entering into the quiet that is
already there—buried under the 50,000 thoughts
the average person thinks every day.

—Deepak Chopra, The Chopra Center (Daily Inspiration Quotes)

CHAPTER ONE
Getting Started

You may have picked up this book for reasons you can't quite articulate. You might feel naturally drawn to exploring meditation and have no particular expectations about where such an inquiry may lead, or what the experience would be like.

It's also possible you have specific reasons for wanting to practice meditation. Maybe you have heard about the various physical, mental, and emotional benefits it can offer: stress relief, relaxation, better sleep, increased intelligence, improved powers of concentration, improved insight and creativity, vibrant energy, and equanimity. Such benefits have been experienced by a long line of practitioners for thousands of years. And more recently, the positive effects of meditation have been scientifically verified. If you're interested in reading those studies, the Institute of Noetic Sciences bibliography

> 66
> *When the mind is at rest, the body is at rest—respiration, heartbeat, and metabolism slow down. Reaching this still point is not something unusual or esoteric. It is an important part of being alive and staying awake. All creatures on the earth are capable of manifesting this stillness.*
>
> —John Daido Loori, *Finding the Still Point*

and the Mindfulness Research Guide (and monthly newsletter) are great resources.

You may have some initial questions, so let's start there.

New Meditators' Questions and Concerns

What Is Meditation?

There are many different forms of meditation. Their common thread is their experiential nature. To really know what meditation is, you have to do it. That said, it can also be useful to have a general sense of what meditation is prior to embarking on your own journey.

Simply put, meditation techniques are tools for knowing, shaping, and liberating the mind. In the same way that cardio or weight-training helps you cultivate a healthy, strong, and flexible body, meditation practice helps you cultivate a healthy, strong, and flexible mind. It also gives you access to a subtle level of awareness (your own inner wisdom), from which you're able to perceive reality directly and with great clarity.

Khandro Rinpoche offers another helpful description of meditation as "a method for breaking down habitual ways of looking at things and for looking at things in a slightly different way." So, for instance, imagine you're in possession of a 108-carat diamond. But the diamond is still encrusted in layers of rock and silt. Here and there, its radiance peeks through, but mostly it looks and feels like a heavy clump of dirt. To reveal the full splendor of the diamond and enjoy all of its qualities, you need to remove those layers of silt and rock.

Meditation practice is similar. The diamond is your inherent, original perfection. It's already present, but it is currently obscured by old mental and emotional habits. Meditation helps reveal the diamond's natural beauty, so your appreciation of it can be more direct and more intimate.

Meditation has both active and receptive aspects. The active aspects have to do with unwinding old perceptual and cognitive patterns and cultivating new ways of seeing. These new ways of seeing are rooted in a quality of detached equilibrium, or benevolent indifference—of giving lots of space to the phenomena of self and world. They also include the development of a form of concentration without fixation. In other words, you learn to focus on objects without grasping them too tightly. You learn to hold them in your attention as you would a beautiful flower in your hand: gently, so as not to crush the stem or petals.

The more receptive aspects of meditation teach you how to relax and listen deeply—to become more sensitive to what's actually happening, inside and out. When a bird lands on the branch outside your window, instead of immediately thinking, *Oh, that's just a bird*, and going back to surfing the Internet, you'll be able to stay with the immediate perception in a way that allows the bird's subtle beauty to become more apparent: the downy-soft feathers on its belly, the sleek beige wing feathers, the way its head tilts, and how its beak quivers in the release of its liltingly harmonious song.

How is meditation different from relaxation?

Meditation is related to relaxation, but with an important difference. For most people, becoming deeply relaxed leads eventually to drowsiness and then sleep. And for most people, being alert is associated with operating in overdrive—in a mode of tense and frenetic rushing around (physically and/or mentally). Meditation is the art of cultivating a state of body-mind that is simultaneously relaxed and alert. In meditation, great ease and great wakefulness live together happily.

How is meditation different from thinking?

There are three aspects of mental functioning you can directly observe: (1) moving mind, (2) still mind, and (3) awareness. Moving mind is the appearance of thoughts, images, sensations, and perceptions. Still mind is the absence of thoughts, images, sensations, and perceptions. Awareness, also called mindfulness, is the part of you that's able to notice or be aware of the moving mind and still mind. Awareness can also be aware of itself—with or without thoughts, images, sensations, and perceptions.

Thinking, then, is simply an aspect of moving mind. Meditation, on the other hand, includes being knowingly tuned into awareness. In other words, when you're meditating, you are aware of the thoughts—rather than simply being drawn along in their stream. You recognize that there's always a part of you that is not thinking. This is the space of pure awareness within which your thoughts arise and dissolve, like clouds passing through the sky.

This awareness is referred to sometimes as Wisdom Mind, universal mind, or big mind. Wisdom Mind is different from conceptual mind (the thinking mind). Conceptual mind believes itself to be separate, limited, and personal. Wisdom Mind knows itself to be unlimited and transpersonal. Wisdom Mind is the electricity that powers the light bulb of conceptual mind. (This subject is discussed further in "Conceptual Mind and Wisdom Mind," page 42.)

Meditation is a tool for plugging into Wisdom Mind, as well as cultivating conceptual mind in ways that render it increasingly bright and pliant.

✱ *Meditation is of two general types: (1) with objects and (2) without objects. Meditation with objects is dualistic, meaning there's a "you" who is meditating and an object that you're focusing on as support for the meditation. For instance, your meditation object may be breath or the flame of a candle. Meditation without objects is nondualistic. In other words, pure awareness shines its light on itself—the seer and the seen are realized to be one and the same.*

How is meditation different from concentration?

Concentration—the capacity to hold attention steady—is one among several skills or qualities that can be cultivated through meditation practice. Other such qualities include clarity, equanimity, energy, confidence, joy, and tranquility. Once developed, these qualities provide nourishment for deeper levels of meditation.

Insight meditation, for instance, includes a focusing of awareness from moment to moment on the ever-changing stream of appearances (e.g., sights, sounds, feelings, thoughts). This sort of mindfulness practice utilizes the mind's capacity to focus one-pointedly (that is, attention rests continuously with clarity and without distraction on a single phenomenon or field of inquiry). What makes it meditation is the delicate dance between mindfulness and concentration—not the concentration in and of itself.

Meditation is for you to realize that the deepest nature of your existence is beyond thoughts and emotions, that it is incredibly vast and interconnected with all other beings.

—Tenzin Palmo, *Cave in the Snow*

CHAPTER TWO

Your First Meditation Session

In this chapter, you'll be introduced to some established guidelines that will help you with your meditation practice, and you'll learn the basics of creating an environment supportive of meditation. Next, you'll be guided through your first one-minute meditation session. Following your first hands-on experience, you'll be introduced to some of the common obstacles to meditation, which you may relate to. Then you'll be provided with answers to frequently asked questions about the meditation process.

Basic Guidelines for Meditation

There are many different types of meditation, each with its own protocols. These guidelines apply to whatever form you happen to be practicing. You will learn about the various forms in later chapters.

Consistency Is Good

Particularly when you're just beginning, it's useful to have a schedule and structure that you commit to. So, for instance, decide that you're going to practice meditation three times a week—Monday, Wednesday, and Friday. Each session will be for ten minutes, from 7:00 to 7:10 a.m. Maintain this schedule for at least three weeks, and then reevaluate.

Wear Loose, Comfortable Clothing

When your body is comfortable, it's easier to relax. Physical relaxation supports mental relaxation—the kind of "letting go" that is an important component of meditation. Choose clothing that doesn't restrict circulation and that gives your skin a sense of being able to breathe (natural fibers are best).

Practice Before a Meal Rather Than After

Most people feel a little drowsy immediately following a meal. The body is in its "rest and digest" mode, so it's best to allow it to do those things. Meditating immediately before a meal is a beautiful way of tuning in to the energy of mindfulness. You may notice that food tastes better after meditating than it does otherwise because of your heightened awareness.

*

Meditation is the art of starting over. *Again and again, you'll notice yourself being distracted during your meditation. This is not a problem. Noticing your distraction is the "magic moment" when you're invited to start over—to knowingly reconnect with awareness. (The "magic moment" will be discussed further in "Sowing the Seeds of Mindfulness," page 41.) Relaxing your jaw completely and saying "ahh" can help you let go of whatever concept, belief, or emotional upheaval you were caught in. Just allow it to pass, and come back to the here and now. Each moment is fresh and new, infinitely rich and mysterious. What is it revealing? Welcome it fully.*

Being Upright

Whether you're sitting on the floor or in a chair, allow your spine to be in its naturally upright position. In this position, your body will feel relaxed and expanded. Also bring your attitude into an upright position. In other words, let your mind be open and alert, cultivate a sense of confidence and curiosity, and know that you're doing something excellent for yourself.

Creating Your Own Peaceful Retreat

Take the time to create home and work environments that are supportive of your meditation practice. You may find that these added measures help you follow through on your intention to meditate. Here are some ideas:

At Home

If possible, practice in a relatively quiet and uncluttered space that is used only for meditation. It does not have to be a separate room; a corner of a room will do. A vase of flowers and a beeswax candle can help create a sense of clarity, peacefulness, and beauty supportive of the internal qualities you wish to cultivate. You may like to use a round meditation cushion (*zafu*), a low-to-ground meditation bench (*seiza* bench), and/or a flat, square meditation pad (*zabuton*) to make sitting more comfortable. You may also sit on a folded blanket or in a straight-backed chair. In any case, leave these props in the meditation space between sessions and treat them with the utmost respect.

At Work

If you have your own office, designate one corner as your meditation space. Keep your meditation props stored in a closet, in your car, or under your desk. You can also practice while sitting right at your desk—no props required. If this is not possible, you can meditate in your car on a cool day or in an empty conference room. Make a habit of devoting the first five minutes of your lunch hour or break time to meditation practice.

On the Go

As you read on, you will discover ways to meditate whenever you feel inspired to, no matter where you are. For instance, the Walking with Mindfulness meditation (discussed in chapter 5) and the Inner Smile meditation (discussed in chapter 6) are excellent techniques for garnering the benefits of this practice. Also, while you are out and about, notice and enjoy spontaneous moments of awareness, of being present, that arise naturally.

Basic One-Minute Meditation: Focus on Breath

Now it's time to get your feet wet with a simple one-minute breathing meditation. For this practice, you'll need a handheld timer (or equivalent app for your tablet or phone) and a chair or cushion to sit on. If you don't yet have a handheld timer, no problem—just use a watch or clock.

✱ *A timer is a beginning meditator's best friend. Continuously checking the time while you're meditating is kind of like glancing at your watch while you're making love—it just doesn't work. You want to be able to give yourself fully to the experience. Knowing that the timer will tell you when the session is over, you're free to engage deeply with the exploration at hand.*

1. Spine Upright

Sit with your spine in its naturally upright position. Feel the support of the floor, chair, or cushion beneath you. Enjoy a couple of deep, slow breaths. With each exhalation, release any tension in your face, neck, jaw, throat, and shoulders. Feel the fluid strength along the vertical centerline of your body, as if there were a column of liquid light flowing just in front of your spine from the tip of your tailbone all the way up to the roof of your mouth. Smile gently. Set your timer for one minute, and press start. Place the timer next to you.

2. Breathe and Count

The technique for this practice is very simple. You're going to tune into the movement of your breath, and then count the inhalations and exhalations, from one to ten, and then start over again at one. Begin by becoming curious about the movement of your breath— feel the inhalations and exhalations flowing into and out of your body, like ocean waves, rising and falling. Feel how your abdomen gently expands and then releases with each round of breathing. Notice that the breath feels cool at your nostrils as it flows in and feels warm at your nostrils as it flows out. And now begin to count the breaths: As you inhale, count "one" (say the number silently to yourself in a gentle, friendly, and matter-of-fact manner). As you exhale, count "two." With the next inhale, count "three." And with the next exhale, count "four." Continue like this until you've reached ten, and then begin at one again. As you count, allow the breath to have its natural rhythm. Make no effort to alter its length or quality. Simply notice its presence, feel it moving in and out of your body, become gently aware of its various qualities, and apply the counting technique.

3. Distraction, Return, Begin Again

If at some point you become distracted—that is, if your mind wanders—notice this has happened (remember, it's the "magic moment") and then begin again with an inhalation counted as "one."

4. Notice How You Feel

When one minute has elapsed, bring the breath-counting practice to a close. Relax. Take note of any feelings or sensations that may have arisen.

Congratulations! You've just completed your first meditation practice. This is wonderful. May it blossom into many more.

Did you make it through a full round of 10 breaths without distraction? If so, that's great. If not, that's great also. Each time you notice you've become distracted and bring yourself gently back to the practice, you're strengthening your "mindfulness muscle." You're nourishing your capacity for concentration and clarity.

When you feel ready, you can increase the amount of time you devote to this practice. One minute can become two minutes, then five,

---

❋ *What's the best way to remember the meditation instructions?* As you approach the exercises in the book, first read through the written instructions for a particular meditation exercise from start to finish. As you read, imagine yourself already doing the practice. Then tune in to the main headings for each step of the practice. These are your "cheat sheets." Perhaps you'll be able to memorize them. If not, you can write the short phrases on a piece of paper to keep nearby and refer to as needed.

ten, thirty, or more. It's up to you. Once you're able to complete several rounds of counting to 10 without distraction (and you have practiced this consistently for at least 10 days), the next step is to count only the exhalations. Let the inhalation unfold without a counting label, then count "one" with the exhalation. Let the next inhalation unfold without a counting label, then count "two" with the next exhalation. Continue in this manner until you've reached 10, and then begin again.

Once you've become comfortable counting just the exhalations (and, again, have practiced this consistently for at least 10 days), you can drop the counting labels entirely, and just notice the inhalations and exhalations themselves. Observe the breath, enjoy the breath, *become the breath*.

Variation

An option for Focus on Breath meditation is to use a *gatha*—a short poem for mindfulness practice, also known as a practice poem—in conjunction with the breathing. This lovely *gatha* by Zen Buddhist monk Thich Nhat Hanh encompasses five rounds of breath:

In, Out

Deep, Slow

Calm, Ease

Smile, Release

Present moment, Wonderful moment.

Recite the first word in the pair with the inhalation and the second word in the pair with the exhalation. As you *inhale*, you say (silently, to yourself), *In*. Then, as you exhale, you say, *Out*. With the next inhale, you say, *Deep*. Then with the exhale, you say, *Slow*. And so on. Repeat the five-line sequence as many times as you'd like or until your timer indicates the time is up.

The Power of a Label

Insight meditation practices (also known as vipassana *in Sanskrit) frequently employ labels—words or phrases that are spoken out loud or recited silently. In breath meditation, you may be instructed to count the inhalations and exhalations, as in the one-minute meditation you tried earlier. The numbers you used to do this are labels. If you're using a gatha, the words of the gatha are labels.*

The purpose of a label is to support conceptual mind in remaining focused on the meditation. Conceptual mind is very good at labeling; it does this for a living. Inviting the mind to participate in the meditation by contributing a label helps it to settle. When conceptual mind feels useful and appreciated, it's less likely to charge off into internal chatter. Instead, it can relax into sweetly focused contentment.

Common Hindrances to Meditation

The vast majority of those who meditate will at some point encounter obstacles. This is not at all unusual, and it's good to know ahead of time what some of the more common hindrances are. This way, you won't be caught off guard when they appear. You'll know that it's a natural part of the process.

Imagine you're the coach of a soccer team, which is scheduled to play a game in the World Cup tournament. You have a very strong team—including both Lionel Messi and Cristiano Ronaldo—but your opponent's team is also strong. So, in preparation for the big game, you send a scout to check out the opposing players—to observe their habitual ways of playing and take stock of their strengths and weaknesses. This is very wise.

Similarly, it's good to know about the hindrances—the opposing players—in your meditation game. You have some excellent players on your home team. The energy of mindfulness is your Lionel Messi, and the interest and enthusiasm you have for meditation is your Cristiano Ronaldo. Nevertheless, even the best players need to rise to the challenges posed by their opponents.

Craving, aversion, laziness, restlessness, and doubt are these opponents. These are negative tendencies that, like being tackled on a soccer field, obstruct your progress. You will learn how to counter each of these tendencies in future chapters (where you'll learn specific meditation practices). Here they'll just be introduced.

Craving

When you've been tackled by a craving, you're convinced that your happiness depends upon possessing an object—and so you crave that thing (or person, or situation). You're sitting on your meditation cushion, and suddenly there arises a nearly irresistible desire to get up and play your favorite video game, turn on the television, eat a pint of Ben and Jerry's ice cream, or maybe even go to the car dealer to test drive that red Porsche you've been lusting after. More subtle cravings include yearning for the bliss of meditative states or creating an idea in your mind about what enlightenment is—and then chasing after it.

Aversion

When you've been tackled by aversion—which is the flip side of craving—you're convinced that your happiness depends on the absence of this or that person, situation, or object. Your mind suggests, with great vigor and eloquence, that if only your legs would stop hurting, you'd be a completely fulfilled human being. If only it weren't so hot in this conference room, your state of calm and clarity would be unsurpassed. If only that person sitting in front of you on the bus would stop twitching and coughing, you'd be well on your way to enlightenment.

Laziness

In some meditation texts, this hindrance is referred to as "sloth." A sloth is a slow-moving mammal native to the jungles of Central and South America. It has long limbs and hooked claws (with either two or three toes) that allow it to hang upside down from the branches of trees. The slowness of sloths, which seems akin to laziness in human eyes, makes their furry coats an ideal habitat for all variety of other organisms: cockroaches, beetles, moths, algae, and fungi. When you've been tackled by sloth, you act like one, deciding that "just hanging out" is much more appealing than sitting on your meditation cushion. Deep within the furry coat of laziness live a variety of other unwholesome states, such as delusion, resentment, frustration, and regret.

Restlessness

When you've been tackled by restlessness, you twitch and squirm and fidget. Your body can't sit still. Your mind is agitated, racing from one thing to the next, like an endless series of television commercials or a continuous cycling through all two hundred of your cable stations. You find it impossible to concentrate for even a nanosecond. You daydream. You feel like you're going to explode. You get up to go to the bathroom, then sit down again. You get up for a drink of water, then sit down again. You go get your phone so you can check your text messages, then sit down again.

Doubt

When you've been tackled by doubt, you question the usefulness of meditation or your capacity to succeed. Or you have doubts about the truth of the teachings. You wonder, *Is this really worth it? Am I doing it right? How do I know that this is the right technique for me? What's the point? Are my teachers trustworthy? Is enlightenment real?* Skepticism and deep questioning can have their place, but if taken to an extreme, they can also be crippling.

Some Questions You May Have Now

How Important Is Posture?

Physical alignment has an effect on the subtle energies of the body—which, in turn, affect the mind. This relationship between subtle energy (*prana*) and mind (*citta*) is the basis for body-centered meditation practices such as qigong, tai chi, and hatha yoga. So do your best to find a posture that feels comfortable and stable and that allows your spine to be in its naturally upright position. This is the most important point.

The position traditionally associated with meditation is lotus pose, which is a rather challenging crossed-legged position with each foot placed on top of the opposite thigh. But there are other seated positions that work equally well. For instance, you can sit cross-legged on a cushion with your knees touching the floor, allowing your hips to be higher than your knees. You can also kneel on the floor while straddling a cushion or stool. (You'll learn more about these postures in chapter 4.)

It's also fine to sit on a straight-backed chair or an ergonomic chair. You can also practice in a standing position. If you're injured or for some other reason unable to sit or stand upright, you can meditate lying down (doing your best to avoid falling asleep).

Should I Meditate with My Eyes Open or Closed?

Either is fine. There are forms of meditation that require the eyes to be open, some that suggest keeping them closed, and others that let you choose. Beginners often find it helpful to keep their eyes closed. Eliminating the barrage of visual stimulation can make it much easier to notice thoughts, internal images, feelings, and bodily sensations.

Eventually, you may wish to integrate visual perception into your meditation for added benefits. But there's no hurry. You can, of course, experiment with both ways of doing it. If you're feeling agitated and distracted, close your eyes and gaze slightly downward along the line of your nose. If you're feeling sleepy, open your eyes and gaze slightly upward and out toward the horizon.

What Should I Do When I Feel Physical Pain During Meditation?

In most forms of meditation, you'll be encouraged to mindfully adjust your posture if you're experiencing painful sensations. In the spirit of nonviolence, do your best to avoid causing harm to your physical body.

It can also be quite interesting to notice the difference between physical sensation and the mental-emotional commentary about the physical sensation. The difference between the two is the difference between physical pain and psychological suffering.

Pain (an unpleasant sensation) is a natural aspect of human experience. Mental-emotional commentary about the pain may or may not arise. If it does arise and you're able simply to witness it—without clinging or repulsion—then it doesn't add insult to injury (so to speak, though in this case also quite literally). If, on the other hand, you "board the train" of this mental-emotional commentary and begin to identify with the thoughts and emotions, the result is psychological suffering. So, though it may seem surprising, the psychological suffering associated with physical pain is actually optional.

With additional guidance, you can learn to create a sense of great spaciousness within which the painful sensations "float." There are also ways of directing breath-energy into the painful areas. These are just two among many meditation techniques that can be used to relate to painful sensations. If so inspired, you can explore these (and others) in more detail. (A good resource is Shinzen Young's *Natural Pain Relief: How to Soothe and Dissolve Physical Pain with Mindfulness.*)

How Long Should I Meditate?

This is entirely up to you. You've already completed a one-minute meditation, which is wonderful. Next time, set your timer for five or ten minutes instead of one and see how that feels. For many of you, fitting a 10-minute meditation into your workday will be fairly easy. But remember: even one minute, or one round of breath, can be a wonderful respite—an opportunity to tap into the peace, joy, and infinite spaciousness that resides, always and already, in the core of your being.

When first establishing a meditation practice, what's most important is consistency. So choose a length of time that feels reasonable and workable, rather than intimidating. Ten minutes three times a week is an excellent goal in the beginning. As you start to experience the benefits of your practice, it will naturally deepen and expand. Let it evolve organically. And enjoy yourself.

Do I Need A Teacher?

Books—like this one and those mentioned in the resources section—can be helpful introductory guides. With a few good written instructions, you can go quite far on your own. The Internet is also an amazing resource; there's so much information available and you'll find some wonderful videos of talks by truly outstanding meditation teachers. (See Video Talks in the resources section, page 164.)

It can also be extremely useful to receive in-person feedback from someone who is farther along the path than you are. A skilled teacher can see clearly where you're still stuck or fooling yourself (for instance, if your "letting go" is actually a "doing nothing"). And group retreats can be a stimulating way to receive the support of a community of practitioners. You may eventually feel drawn to connect with a community or teacher in this way.

My Mind/Emotions Are Getting More, Not Less, Agitated. What's That All About?

For new meditators, a very common experience is to feel like meditation is making things worse, rather than better. Suddenly, your mind seems absolutely riotous—a churning waterfall of thoughts and emotions. Certainly it wasn't like this before?! What's actually happening is that you're just noticing, for the first time, the mental antics that previously had been operating mostly behind the scenes. Now that you've learned how to shine the light of awareness on the contents of your mind, you can actually see these patterns of thought, image, and emotion.

This added clarity is not bad news. In fact, it's really good news! To be mindful of thoughts in this way—that is, to notice you're *having* thoughts—is actually a profound insight. Before now, you habitually identified with the thoughts. In other words, you just assumed you *were* the thoughts. Now you've tuned into an aspect of yourself that can simply witness the thoughts. Suddenly, there's space between "you" as the observer of the thoughts and the thoughts themselves.

And this is quite interesting: Who or what is it that's *seeing* the thoughts?

Does Meditation Mean Escaping from the World?

It's a common misconception to think that people who meditate are just trying to escape from the world or ignore reality. It's actually just the opposite. Meditation is not an escape, but rather the ultimate confrontation with reality. The sensitivity and uncensored perception cultivated through meditation allow you to interact with the things and people of the world much more authentically and intimately.

Sitting in silence does require a certain kind of solitude, particularly in the beginning stages. You're learning to turn your attention inward, rather than habitually directing it outward. Isolating yourself—for a certain amount of time—from the usual barrage of sensory stimulation tends to be really helpful. But try not to think of this as an escape, rather as quiet time to tenderly embrace, in the arms of truth, all that is arising.

✳ *From suffering to freedom. In Buddhism, the term* samsara *is used to describe the dissatisfaction and suffering that result from seeing the world through the lens of an ignorant and agitated mind. The term* nirvana *points to the freedom from such suffering. The meditation teacher Tulku Urgyen Rinpoche, as quoted in* The Healing Power of Meditation, *wrote: "Samsara is mind turned outwardly, lost in its projections. Nirvana is mind turned inwardly, recognizing its nature." In other words, peace and happiness come from shining the light of awareness on the contents of your mind (its various thoughts, emotions, and sensations) and then realizing that who you are essentially is this light of awareness.*

petty ego/NAFS/rat mind
cf Supreme lens

When meditation is mastered,
the mind is unwavering like the flame
of a lamp in a windless place.

—Krishna, *Bhagavad Gita 6:19*

CHAPTER THREE

A Light and Simple Approach

Now that you've learned a bit about what meditation is, you're ready to explore the meditation process more deeply. In this chapter, you'll be given guidance on how best to approach your meditation practice. You'll discover how the brief 10-minute meditations in this book can be wonderful tools for calming the mind. You'll be alerted to potential obstacles and wrong turns, and you'll learn how to avoid these pitfalls or rectify them. You'll also learn more about how meditation can contribute to happiness.

Relieving Suffering and Creating Happiness

If you look closely, you'll find that your reasons for doing anything can usually be boiled down to a desire to (1) relieve suffering and (2) create happiness. It can be interesting, as you go through your day, to pause occasionally and ask yourself, *Why am I doing this?* If, for instance, you happen to be scrambling eggs for breakfast, ask yourself, *Why am I cooking these eggs?* The answer will most likely have to do with relieving hunger and creating the sense of satisfaction that comes from a tasty meal and full belly.

Similarly, your reasons for learning meditation are likely some variation on the themes of relieving suffering and creating happiness. This is natural and a very good thing. As you go deeper into the practice, you'll learn more about this motivation, this natural draw toward happiness. For now, try to clarify for yourself what your hopes and expectations are regarding meditation—and examine whether, in some way or another, they have to do with becoming happier, more peaceful, and more joyful.

> 66
>
> *In meditation, we are in a state of restful alertness that is extremely refreshing for the body and mind. As people stick with their meditation ritual, they notice that they are able to accomplish more while doing less. Instead of struggling so hard to achieve goals, they spend more and more time 'in the flow'—aligned with universal intelligence that orchestrates everything.*
>
> —Deepak Chopra, "Seven Myths of Meditation"

A Direct Experience

Your foray into learning about the practice of meditation could be compared with going on a vacation—let's say, taking a two-week trip to Paris. In preparation for the trip, you create an itinerary—a general plan for where you'll go and what you'll see. You also collect the various maps to help you find the Eiffel Tower or guide you in the surrounding countryside.

The itinerary and maps are useful. The real joy of the vacation, however, comes from your direct experience of Paris and the French countryside. It comes from the fragrance of almond croissants when you pass the patisserie early in the morning as the sun is rising; when people of all ages are passing by and speaking a language

you only faintly understand. It comes from finding a gently slop-
ing field of sunflowers, which you decide to wander through as you
nibble on your warm almond croissant. It comes from the sweetly
spontaneous conversations you have with your travel partner, the
shared love, and unexpected moments of intimacy.

The direct experience of the patisserie and the sunflower field
is not something that can be seen on a map. The specifics of this
(or any) experience cannot be anticipated by an itinerary. In fact,
the true richness of life—what is most deeply satisfying—emerges
precisely in the moments of letting go of your maps and itineraries.
It's when you release your expectations and welcome fully what's
actually happening that the true reason for taking the vacation
becomes apparent.

66
*If your mind is empty, it is always ready for anything; it is
open to everything. In the beginner's mind there are many
possibilities; in the expert's mind there are few.*

—Shunryu Suzuki, *Zen Mind, Beginner's Mind*

The same is true for meditation practice. While there are useful
maps and itineraries, the deepest benefits emerge in moments of
dropping all goals and expectations. This is one of the paradoxes
of meditation practice. The effort you apply will be of a special
kind, infused with a sense of openness and release. How exactly it
unfolds will differ from person to person. It's your journey, and no
one else's. As you begin this journey, here are some tips that may
be useful:

- In a certain sense, learning to meditate is similar to cultivating any skill. It may feel a bit awkward in the beginning. As it becomes more familiar, there will be a kind of momentum that supports you. Even so, there will be ups and downs, moments of ease and moments of difficulty. This is natural.

- Do your best to replace heavy expectations (for instance, "I want to feel ecstatically blissful 24/7" or "I want all my problems to be gone completely and forever") with gentle, clear intentions ("May my practice support ease and clarity"). Then remember that such intentions are just the trip itinerary. Let them serve their purpose without granting them undue importance. Drop them lightly—like the seeds of a flower—into the energy of your heart-space (that place inside you where love and compassion dwell). Water them every now and again, and make sure they get sufficient sunlight. Trust that time and nature will do the rest—as you fully enjoy each moment of the journey.

- When you notice yourself yearning for some future goal, stop and redirect that constricted "seeking" energy into being more deeply focused on what's happening in the moment, the right now.

- Replace the notion of "control" with that of "influence." As you meditate, take the stance of a surfer, leaning this way or that way on your board. There's no thought of controlling the wave. Instead, you're just skillfully riding it.

- Do your best to stay connected to the beginner's mind: a sense of freshness, innocence, wonder, and awe. See through the eyes of a visitor from another planet, gazing upon the earth for the very first time. When you view the world without preconceived notions, you'll be inclined to exclaim, "How awesome!"

> 66
>
> *In practicing meditation, we're not trying to live up to some kind of ideal—quite the opposite. We're just being with our experience, whatever it is.*
>
> —Pema Chödrön, *When Things Fall Apart*

Befriending the Monkey Mind

As you sit down to meditate and turn your attention inward, you're likely to encounter what is fondly known as the "monkey mind." Thoughts, images, and emotions will be jumping around like a troop of excited monkeys, swinging from branches and leaping into the air, each with its own agenda.

You may feel surprised, and perhaps a bit disheartened, to find such chaos within your mind. Please understand that such an experience is very common; almost all meditators experience something similar, at least initially. Becoming curious about and familiar with the monkey mind is an important first step.

As you begin to pay closer attention to this rather incoherent jumble of thoughts, images, and sensations, certain patterns will become apparent. What you'll likely notice is that a large percentage of these thoughts and feelings revolve around the themes of past and future. They're ruminations, regrets, or fond memories of the past, alternating with fears, expectations, or plans for the future.

You may also notice that much of the content of the monkey mind comprises (1) thoughts about things you don't have now but want (a new car, maybe even a red Porsche) and how to get them, and (2) thoughts about things you do have now but don't want (the flu or a job you hate) and how to get rid of them. Once again, this is not at all unusual.

It's also good to know that thoughts are not inherently bad. Certain thoughts are genuinely useful and/or enjoyable, and they can be honored and respected as such. There are thoughts, for instance, that have to do with accomplishing practical tasks, such as thinking about what time the post office closes or which bus you need to take to arrive on time for your acupuncture appointment. There are thoughts that are beautifully creative, like the thinking process of a mathematician, a philosopher, or a physicist, or the thoughts involved in planning how to arrange your flower garden, what color to paint the walls in your new house, or which hors d'oeuvres would be best to serve at your daughter's wedding reception. There are thoughts that are inherently nourishing and enjoyable, like remembering a genuine act of kindness received or offered. And there are thoughts that are useful to us as meditators, like recalling instructions, using thought to count breaths, and so on.

Monkey mind is none of these. Instead, it is the mental chattering that seems to be largely random, utterly lacking in rhyme or reason. Here are some typical qualities of monkey-mind thoughts, images, and feelings, as well as how a meditation practice can soften their edges:

Chaotic and Scattered

Monkey-mind thoughts tend to be scattered and confused, incoherent and messy.

Imagine: The thought-monkeys are jumping from branch to branch, scattering leaves, and making a mess, with no obvious attempt to form meaningful connections with one another. It's anarchy, pure and simple.

How meditation helps

Over time, meditation cultivates a sense of spaciousness and calm in the mind, allowing this chaos to settle. Your thinking processes become more organized and clear.

Aggressive and Demanding

When your thought processes are filled with anger and aggression, this also is a sign of the monkey mind.

In terms of our monkey-mind metaphor: The thought-monkeys are at war with one another, screeching and scratching and throwing coconuts. They form alliances, perform elaborate flank attacks, make demands, and unceremoniously decline all suggestions of a cease-fire.

How meditation helps

Over time, meditation cultivates a sense of equanimity, providing a soothing balm for such coarse, aggressive energy. Your thinking becomes more spacious, creative, gentle, and kind.

Whiny, Wilted, and Sleepy

If you're in the habit of feeling defeated or victimized by life, you're likely ensnared in some variety of the monkey mind.

Imagine each thought as a monkey: The thought-monkeys are complaining, feeling victimized by pretty much everything. They're casting blame and feeling shame. They retreat into resignation, subterranean grumbling, and restless sleep.

How meditation helps

With continued meditation practice, your thinking becomes less foggy and confused, revealing a mind that's naturally fluid and light, energetic and buoyant.

Sneaky and Fearful

The thought-monkeys' teeth are chattering. They huddle together, terrified. They sneak and they scheme, convinced that the world and all its inhabitants are dangerous.

One sure sign of monkey-mind activity is persistent feelings of fear, dread, foreboding, or impending doom.

How meditation helps

Meditation helps you to see the thought patterns (the unexamined storylines, beliefs, and assumptions) that trigger emotional reactivity. As these old patterns dissolve, a sense of confidence and ease naturally emerges. This, in turn, supports you in going even deeper into the investigation, unraveling even more subtle patterns. Eventually, the core fear—the fear of death—is faced and dissolved, revealing what is known as the "deathless" or "unborn" realm of infinite freedom.

Repetitive and Boring

The thought-monkeys seem to be caught in an endless loop, an infinite replay of a really bad movie. *Can someone please change the channel?*

If you look closely, you'll likely find thought patterns that appear again and again. Some of these may be useful, but many are simply obsessive monkey-mind thoughts that can be released to create space for more original, creative thinking . . . or just silence.

How meditation helps

Habitual thought patterns are correlated with pathways in the brain—neural networks that have become deeply grooved. Meditation helps you replace these old, boring ruts—those ways of thinking that keep you numb and confused—with fresh, new pathways. Think of a footpath through a grassy field. When it's used frequently, it becomes deep and wide. When it's no longer used, it soon becomes overgrown with grass and eventually merges back into the field. Similarly, a habitual thought pattern, say the habit of judging (e.g., "This person is bad or wrong, because . . .") dissolves once you start walking on a different path. Meditation helps you create these alternative pathways; they become new ways of traveling through your sensory and cognitive fields.

You may discover additional characteristics that are unique to your own troop of monkeys, your own monkey-mind thinking. Chances are good, however, that a majority of what happens within the jungle of your monkey mindscape will be chaotic and scattered; aggressive and demanding; whiny, wilted, and sleepy; sneaky and fearful; and/or repetitive and boring.

As you begin to see this clearly, you may find yourself having a good chuckle over the antics of the monkey mind. The situation is both funny and sad. Such tremendous energy is being invested in producing uninspiring and irritating "movies," one after another. What a bizarre situation! The good news is: Meditation helps.

The Ephemeral Nature of Thoughts

There's one more quality of monkey-mind thoughts that overlaps all the others and is important enough to merit special treatment. This is the quality of being ephemeral. What does this mean? It means that the thoughts, images, and emotions are impermanent. They come and go, arise and dissolve continuously, in a kaleidoscopic and dreamlike fashion. Even those endlessly repetitive thoughts, taken individually, are just momentary appearances. You can confirm this for yourself.

Begin by asking yourself, *Where do these thoughts come from? And where do they go once they've disappeared? Where do the internal images come from? And where do they go once they've disappeared? Where do the emotions come from? And where do they go once they've disappeared?*

These are interesting questions to explore. You can make this a more active process by trying the Cat-and-Mouse Experiment.

The Cat-and-Mouse Experiment

Imagine you're a cat, crouching right outside a mouse hole, waiting patiently for the mouse to emerge (so that you can engage in friendly play, of course). Apply this same attitude to the question, "What is my next thought going to be?" Assume the mental stance of a cat, waiting to see what thought pops up next. As it emerges, like a mouse from its mysterious hole, try to catch the thought (see it clearly) before it vanishes back into the hole. Then wait for the next "mouse" to appear, again trying to see it clearly. Do this a few more times to experience how quickly individual thoughts come and go. You'll see that there's a never-ending stream of mice coming and going. You may also notice that the very act of watching carefully for them (in your friendly cat stance) tends to make them a bit more timid.

As you become more familiar with the contents of your monkey mind, you can begin to notice when it's extremely active, when it's moderately active, and when it's inactive. In other words, you can notice when your mind is moving and when your mind is still. In both cases, there is also an *awareness* of that movement or stillness. So there are three main players you can identify: (1) moving mind, (2) still mind, and (3) awareness. Tuning into and refining the *awareness* component is also known as developing *mindfulness*—which is a primary focus of the practices discussed in this book.

Certain meditation practices are concerned primarily with the *content* or *status* of the mind—that is, whether it's moving or still and what kinds of thoughts and images are appearing (and then disappearing) within the moving mind. Other meditation practices are more interested in the *nature* of mind—with the awareness of awareness itself. In the latter approach, pure awareness, or the container for the various contents of mind, is explored directly. The practices in this book will support you in both of these explorations.

The Myth of "Mind Control"

A common misunderstanding about meditation is that it is about controlling thoughts and feelings. According to this mistaken belief, you're able to decide which thoughts and feelings you want and which you don't want, and then use meditation techniques to execute something of a coup d'etat, replacing the old evil regime (of bad thoughts and unpleasant feelings) with the new enlightened one (of good thoughts and pleasant feelings).

Now, there is a kind of influencing—a cultivation of the mind in a positive, wholesome direction—that is possible and desirable. After all, what reason would there be to meditate if not for an outcome that is in some way beneficial? The mistake lies in the hidden assumption of a limited and separate self (ego)—an unchanging and identifiable "me"—who is the chooser of the thoughts and feelings and their subsequent owner. Believing that you can choose your individual thoughts and feelings tends to reinforce this notion of a separate "me" who's in control of things—a trap that is best avoided.

Take a minute or two, right now, to tune in to your internal screen upon which thoughts and images are appearing. Simply notice the various thoughts and images that are arising: some of past events, some of imagined future events, and many that are completely dreamlike and chaotic. Does it really make sense to say that you are choosing these thoughts? Not really. See this clearly. For the most part, thoughts appear in pretty much the same way the weather does. They just arrive from who knows where.

Now, you may reply, *Well, if I'm not choosing these thoughts, who is?* And the answer is: no one. No one *in particular*, that is. An equally valid answer is: the entire universe. This is a lot to grasp early on in your journey, but really try to take this in: Each thought is a wave, emerging from the ocean of reality, whose causes and conditions are limitless. At this particular space-time location, the entire universe is appearing as this thought.

There is no personal thinker of the thoughts. There's just thinking. It's just the ocean playfully waving. When you really see this, it will be an "aha" moment that will feel deeply liberating. Until then, simply take it on as a hypothesis. Be open to the possibility that this is actually how it is—that the monkey-mind movies are just that: movies. And that the "chooser" of the movies is Universal Studios: the universe. The only sense in which "you" are choosing the thoughts is in the sense of you as the universe: the *You-niverse*. Now enjoy your popcorn!

Granted, there are some thoughts that seem to be more consciously chosen. If, for instance, someone says to you, "Think of a pink elephant," you can project an image of a pink elephant. If someone asks you where in your kitchen you keep the bottle opener, you can project an internal map of the kitchen layout to support you in answering. If you're a writer teasing out the plot development for your next novel, you're able to create such thought patterns. But what's also true is that the "you" who is *apparently* creating these thoughts is simultaneously being created moment by moment.

But these thoughts are not the sort a meditation practice is primarily concerned with. Instead, it's the monkey mind that is the initial realm of inquiry. It's the monkey-mind thoughts that, if granted a command function, create all kinds of problems. These are also the thoughts that tend to be most embarrassing, most frustrating, most annoying, and most incomprehensible. So it's actually really good news to know that you are not choosing them. Like the weather, they're just appearing.

What's even better news is to know that you can cultivate a way of relating to these monkey-mind thoughts that minimizes the havoc they wreak.

At this point, then, what's most important to understand is that the problem is not with the thoughts and feelings themselves, but rather in how you habitually relate to them. When you believe that the thoughts and feelings define who you are, then you're more likely to be drawn into push-pull dynamics—that is, caught within the storyline of their drama. So, please remember, as Tilopa, the Tibetan meditation master (www.thewayofmeditation.com), has said, "The appearances of the world are not the problem, it's clinging to them that causes suffering."

Instead of rejecting or clinging to thoughts, imagine thoughts and feelings as a train coming into a station. You're standing on the landing as the train comes in, draws to a halt, and then opens its doors. At this point, you have a choice: You can either board the train, or you can say, "No, thanks," and just remain on the station platform as it departs. It's the same with thoughts and feelings.

When they appear in your mind, you can "board the train"—following the thoughts as they unfold their storyline—or you can choose to remain on the platform, watching as the thought-train disappears into the distance.

Avoiding Monkey-Mind Pitfalls

Once you've taken a clear look at the antics of the monkey mind, you're at an important juncture. At this point, there are a couple of common wrong turns new meditators make, which will be good for you to avoid. These "mistakes" are based upon the myth that meditators are able to control their thoughts and feelings, as discussed earlier.

Wrong Turn #1

In seeing the chaotic, aggressive, confused, or just downright silly jumble of thoughts and feelings, you think, *Since this is my mind that's such a mess, it must mean that I personally am bad, wrong, or in some way deficient.* You feel guilty for the kinds of thoughts appearing in the monkey mindscape.

Resolution

Understand that you—as an individual, separate person—are not "choosing" the thoughts. Thoughts appear in the way the weather does. When there's a thunderstorm raging outside, it would never occur to you to think, *I must be a bad person since this thunderstorm is now appearing in the environment outside my window.* Monkey-mind thoughts and emotions are the "weather" of your internal environment; that's all. Don't take it personally!

Wrong Turn #2

Having seen the wildness of monkey-mind thoughts, you decide to apply forceful effort to repress or change the thoughts. As a first step, you solidify your notion of "me." In other words, you contract into a muscle-bound, iron-fisted "me" whose new mission in life is to domesticate the wild thoughts, using whatever forceful or manipulative means might be required.

Resolution

Understand that such an iron-fisted approach will be completely counterproductive. In fact, it's likely to just make the "problem" worse. Make no effort to forcefully change what is arising within the monkey mindscape. Remember, it's just the weather. But understand that where you do have a choice (and where your freedom lies) is in *how you relate* to the monkey-mind thoughts. You can choose via the energy of mindfulness to avoid being drawn into their storylines.

When you make this choice to just acknowledge the thoughts, instead of being sucked into emotional reactivity, you're embodying the wisdom of an Aikido master, who fully receives the energy of their opponent, and then transforms it to their advantage. The energy of mindfulness is your internal Aikido master; it knows exactly what to do with the energy of monkey-mind thinking. Over time, with this Aikido-like approach, the general contours of the monkey mindscape will indeed transform in beneficial ways. But it can't be forced.

Sowing the Seeds of Mindfulness

So how exactly do you go about cultivating this energy of mindfulness that will provide the guidance of an "internal Aikido master"?

The first step is to understand the difference between conceptual mind and Wisdom Mind. The next step is to start tuning in to and appreciating "magic moments"—when the energy of mindfulness arrives on the scene. As these "magic moments" become more frequent and the energy of mindfulness flows more continuously, you'll be able to enjoy its benefits in all aspects of your life.

Conceptual Mind and Wisdom Mind

There is an important distinction between conceptual mind and Wisdom Mind. In this book, these terms will be used in the following way: Conceptual mind is your thinking mind. It's the mind that uses language (words and images) and logic. It's the mind that knows things by understanding them intellectually. Conceptual mind includes practical thoughts, creative thoughts, and monkey-mind thoughts.

Wisdom Mind, on the other hand, is the source of intuition—an immediate, direct, and nonverbal sort of knowing. It's not bound by the rules of logic and doesn't speak in any particular human language. Wisdom Mind arrives as the visceral understanding of an "aha" moment or the sense of being overwhelmed by beauty or touched by an act of kindness. It can feel a bit like falling in love with no one in particular—sweetly expansive, deeply relaxing, and vivid in a way that perpetually eludes description. It's also utterly simple: You tune into it simply by paying attention to the aware presence that's associated with the words "I am."

The difference between Wisdom Mind and conceptual mind is something like the difference between electricity and a light bulb. Electricity is the power that allows a bulb to emit light. The light bulb, with its filament, provides a vehicle through which electricity becomes visible. While light bulbs are visible and have specific locations, electricity itself is invisible and nonlocal. While there is a multitude of light bulbs, there's just a single field of electricity that empowers them all.

In this metaphor, electricity is akin to Wisdom Mind and the light bulb to conceptual mind. The brightness of the bulb—how powerfully and transparently it transmits the electricity to illuminate a particular room—can be likened to a person's degree of mindfulness. Mindfulness is the transparent functioning of Wisdom Mind through a human being.

The Magic Moment

As explained, the word *mindfulness* refers to the functioning of Wisdom Mind—the brightness of the lamp of your awareness. Mindfulness can be contrasted to distraction. To be distracted means to be caught up in the dramas of monkey mind. It means you've "boarded the train" of your thoughts, images, and emotions, and you are being taken for a ride. Ten minutes, an hour, two hours later, you may suddenly pop out of that waking dream—realizing only then that you've just spent all that time embroiled in a fantasy, a fictionalized world of your own (largely unconscious) making.

✳ **Don't worry if there is thinking.** *Thinking is not an obstacle, provided you don't believe what you think. The thought, "I am a person; I need this; I don't like that" is not a problem at all unless you think it's true. This thought is like the con artist trying to sell you a vacuum cleaner for $999. It's fine unless you believe his sales pitch.*

—Francis Lucille, unpublished transcript
(www.francislucille.com)

This moment of realizing that you've been distracted is called the "magic moment." It's magical because in the moment of realizing that you've been distracted, you're no longer distracted. So it's a moment to be celebrated!

How to Plant Seeds of Mindfulness

In moments of mindfulness, you're seeing reality exactly as it is, rather than as it appears through the filter of the monkey mind. In these moments, thoughts, perceptions, and sensations are perceived clearly. When you're seeing in a mindful way, you are aware of the individual characteristics of what's occurring, while at the same time being aware of their impermanent nature. In other words, you perceive how the objects of self and world are continuously transforming, while also appreciating the vividness with which they appear.

Here are two good ways to plant seeds of mindfulness:

- Explore the various practices offered in this book.
- Experiment with perceiving "nakedly," with bare attention, by letting go of judgments, explanations, and concepts. When you're looking at a tree, for instance, stay with the immediate perceptions and sensations: the shape and color of the leaves, the feeling of the breeze on your cheek, the sound of birdsong emerging from its branches. If you notice yourself spinning off into a storyline (for example, "This tree reminds me of the first date with my first girlfriend, 10 years ago, when we were walking in the park . . ."), gently bring yourself back to being aware of shapes, colors, and sounds of the here and now. (When you're ready, there's more on "getting naked" in chapter 7.)

> * *Mindfulness is cultivated by a gentle effort, by effortless effort. The meditator cultivates mindfulness by constantly reminding himself in a gentle way to maintain his awareness of whatever is happening right now. Persistence and a light touch are the secrets. Mindfulness is cultivated by constantly pulling oneself back to a state of awareness, gently, gently, gently.*
>
> —Henepola Gunaratana,
> *Mindfulness in Plain English*

When Mindfulness Blossoms

As mentioned above (it bears repeating!): In moments of mindfulness, you're seeing reality exactly as it is, rather than as it appears through the filter of the monkey mind. In such moments of mindfulness, self and world arise without distortion, i.e., free from the storylines associated with monkey mind. They're seen for what they are. A poetic way of expressing this is to say that you're "shining the light of mindfulness" upon the contents of experience.

You can shine the light of mindfulness upon physical sensations such as the breath, upon the perceptions of the external world such as a tree, upon thoughts and internal images, and upon emotional feelings. You can shine the light of mindfulness upon various mental-emotional processes such as the process by which you construct your notion of self—the idea of "me." You can also shine the light of mindfulness upon awareness itself—"awareness of awareness." The benefits are truly endless:

- When mindfulness of physical sensations begins to blossom, your physical body "comes alive" with increasing sensitivity.

When it blossoms fully, the experience of solidity is replaced by the experience of flowing, subtle energy, and vast spaciousness.

- When mindfulness of perception begins to blossom, you start to see things in a fresh new way and appreciate them more deeply. When it blossoms fully, your world becomes filled with beauty.

- When mindfulness of thoughts and internal images begins to blossom, you're able more clearly to view the "internal movies" that you're projecting, and you become curious about creating new ones. When it blossoms fully, your mind becomes filled with truth.

- When mindfulness of feelings begins to blossom, you're able and willing to welcome, with benevolent indifference, whatever emotions are arising. When it blossoms fully, your heart becomes filled with love.

- When mindfulness of awareness begins to blossom, you become more curious about the aware presence that is the "witness" of thoughts, perceptions, and feelings. When it blossoms fully, you become awake to the deepest level of reality and realize your true identity to be Wisdom Mind—the unlimited and transpersonal pure awareness that transcends space and time (and which is none other than the awareness that is "aware of" these words, right now).

Learning to Let Go

To "let go" of a perception, thought, or feeling means to allow the thought or feeling to arise and dissolve in its own time. It means to adopt an attitude similar to the sky's attitude toward clouds. The sky simply allows clouds to form, transform, and dissolve without interfering in any way. You can also, in a sky-like fashion, allow perceptions, thoughts, and feelings to arise and dissolve without interfering with them.

The kind of interference you'll be letting go of typically comes in one of three varieties: (1) grasping, (2) rejection, and (3) ignorance. When you grasp at a perception, thought, or feeling, you try to hold it tightly, pull it closer to you, and prevent it from leaving. When you reject a perception, thought, or feeling, you try to push it away and get rid of it forcefully. When you ignore a perception, thought, or feeling, you numb out the part of you that might perceive it, pretending that it's not really happening.

To be in the space of "letting go" means resisting the temptation to indulge in grasping, rejection, or ignorance. It means being the sky, granting absolute freedom to the clouds.

The Difference Between "Letting Go" and "Doing Nothing"

In a certain sense, letting go could be described as doing nothing. When you allow perceptions, thoughts, and feelings to arise and dissolve without interference—welcoming them fully into the space of awareness—what you're *not doing* is engaging in the push-pull dynamics of grasping, rejection, and ignorance.

What you *are doing*, however, is gently maintaining the light of mindfulness and/or awareness. What you *are also doing* is releasing any impulse to indulge in grasping, rejection, and ignorance.

There's also a kind of "doing nothing" that is no more than laziness. It's an unconscious resistance or collapse that is simply a form of ignorance. This is the sort of doing nothing that says, "Why should I meditate when I can watch TV instead?" This laziness may masquerade as letting go—that is, as enlightened laziness. Don't be fooled.

There's a related sort of "doing nothing" characterized by a secretly rigid laissez-faire attitude of noninterference. This is a crude and lazy indifference that says, "Oh, whatever—it really doesn't matter what thoughts and emotions are arising or whether I pay attention to them—it's all good." But the truth is that it actually does matter, particularly at the beginning and intermediate levels of meditation. It's only by systematically paying attention to your thoughts that you're able to cultivate mindfulness: the capacity to make your stand as the awareness that notices the thoughts, rather than being swept away by their dramas.

Once such mindfulness has been cultivated and deepened, you can then move to the next stage of the process—which is to notice that the thoughts are actually made of awareness. In the same way that the true substance of waves is water, the true substance of each and every thought is awareness. Once this understanding has ripened, it's no longer necessary to be quite as vigilant about maintaining an attitude of mindfulness. But for beginners, the effort to distinguish thoughts from awareness is important; it's not a step that can be skipped. (For more on this process, see the introduction to the Flowing into the Gap meditation on page 132.)

When to Let Go of Old Recipes for Happiness

One of the sad ironies of human existence is that we all want to be happy, yet so often we act in ways that create suffering. We do this because many of our recipes for happiness are deeply flawed. For example, let's say that your great-great-grandmother had a truly excellent recipe for chocolate cake, which called for three bars of dark Belgian chocolate. But somewhere along the way, through an innocent translation error, "three bars of Belgian chocolate" became "thirteen bars of Belgian chocolate." Again and again you follow this recipe—handed down to you as a precious family heirloom—and again and again it creates suffering (serious indigestion) instead of happiness.

What does this have to do with letting go? As you learn to let go, or to release habitual patterns of grasping, rejection, and ignorance, your body and mind become deeply relaxed. From within this space of abiding calmness, you're able to see more clearly the workings of cause and effect, and you gain insight into what lies beyond cause and effect. In particular, you're able to understand, more clearly and directly, what causes suffering and to identify the source of true and lasting happiness.

These new insights allow you to replace ineffective recipes for happiness (however hallowed they may be) with more effective ones. Suddenly, it becomes quite apparent to you that adding 13 bars of chocolate to your cake batter is not a recipe for happiness. You try using fewer bars of Belgian chocolate, and things are better.

It's also useful to understand that "letting go" does not necessarily imply the absence of external action. Letting go of habitual

Make an Inventory of Your Recipes for Happiness

Your personal recipes for happiness are the strategies you've adopted from your parents, your teachers, your sports heroes, your financial advisor, the media, or whomever. These recipes may be perfectly good ones, or they may be flawed. So, try this: Take out a piece of paper or open a word processing file. Then complete the sentence that begins "I will be happy if . . . " Repeat this process, listing sentences, one after another, saying what you believe will make you happy. Then, go back over what you've written and ask yourself: Which of these recipes are reliable and which are not? Which are actually bearing fruit (that is, supporting lasting peace and happiness)? Which are causing bouts of indigestion? *Be honest in your answers.*

grasping, rejection, and ignorance is an internal movement of mind that allows you to see more clearly. From the space of such clarity, external actions may or may not emerge. You can be engaged fully in a variety of external actions, while maintaining a meditator's stance of "letting go." This is actually the secret of supremely effective action.

If, at any point along your journey, you feel uncertain about whether your (external or internal) "doing nothing" is authentic "letting go," or if it's just some form of laziness in disguise, it would be a good idea to consult a teacher. Continue with your meditation practice, however, as the difference may eventually become apparent to you.

Three General Approaches for Letting Go of Unproductive Thoughts, Beliefs, and Attitudes

1. **Replace the unproductive thought or attitude with a more productive one.** If, for instance, you're feeling intensely jealous of a coworker who just received a promotion, replace that feeling of jealously with a sense of sympathetic joy—of being genuinely happy for the success of your coworker. (For specifics on how to do this later in your process, see the Sympathetic Joy meditation, page 109.)

2. **Be the sky through which the thought or attitude is floating like a cloud.** In the example above, allow the feeling of jealousy to arise, notice how it shifts and changes, notice any patterns that emerge, and then watch it dissolve. (For specifics on how to do this later in your process, see the Letting Go of Thoughts meditation, page 60.)

3. **See the inherent purity of the thought or attitude.** This is
    less of an explicit technique and more of a view that can
    be adopted, as well as the natural fruit of a more advanced
    meditation practice. You relate to the jealousy as a form of
    subtle energy and tune in to its inherent luminosity. It's just
    a modulation of the natural brightness of your mind, like a
    ripple on the surface of a shining pond. (Don't worry too much
    about this one at this point in your journey. You may, however,
    catch glimpses of it in the Flowing into the Gap and Getting
    Naked meditations, pages 132 and 141.)

PART TWO

The Practice of Meditation

Just go into the room, sit in the center of the room, open the doors and windows, and see who comes to visit. You will witness all kinds of scenes and actors, all kinds of temptations and stories, everything imaginable. Your only job is to stay in your seat. You will see it all arise and pass, and out of this, wisdom and understanding will come.

—Ajahn Chah, *The Teachings of Ajahn Chah*

CHAPTER FOUR
Sitting Meditation

As its name implies, sitting meditation is meditating in a seated position. The particular posture you assume is less important than the general principle, which is simply to allow the physical body to be still for a while. When you sit still, say during a 10-minute meditation break during a stressful day, your mind is naturally refreshed. During longer sitting meditation periods, your body goes into "rest and repair" mode and receives many of the same benefits of a good night's sleep.

With the physical body relatively still, you're able to notice more subtle movements of energy and mind. More refined perceptions and insights come quite naturally to the fore. Think of being in a room with the loud drone of an air conditioner. Its sound dominates the field of your hearing. Now imagine turning off the air conditioner. Suddenly, you notice the tick tock of a clock, which previously was lost within the continuous hum of the air conditioner. Stop the clock, and you now become aware of the sound of your breathing.

Sitting meditation works in a similar way. You arrange the bones and muscles of your physical body in a way that supports the cessation of coarse levels of movement. This allows you to start noticing other things: the rhythm of your breath, the beating of your heart, sensations of subtle energy, and thoughts arising and dissolving within your mind. Then you begin to notice the one who is noticing. *Who is that?*

The essential process of sitting meditation can happen also while you're standing or lying down. So if you have an injury or illness that prevents you from being able to sit comfortably, no problem. Find a posture that works for you.

It's good to alternate sitting meditation practice with moving meditation of some sort: yoga, qigong, tai chi, and walking meditation are all excellent options. Over time, these contemplative movement practices will help make your sitting more comfortable. They will also provide a means by which the insights of your sitting practice can be incorporated fully into every organ, bone, and cell of your precious human body. (There's more on this topic in chapter 5.)

Setting Up for Your Sitting Meditation

As you explore sitting meditation, you'll discover which positions are most comfortable for you. If your hips are fairly flexible, you may choose to sit directly on the floor. (For a discussion of the props for comfortably meditating in a seated position, see "Creating Your Own Peaceful Retreat," page 13.)

Several positions work particularly well for sitting meditation. Both their English names and Sanskrit names are provided here so that you can begin familiarizing yourself with some of the language you'll encounter during your meditation journey. These include:

- Easy Pose (*Sukhasana*)
- Hero Pose (*Virasana*)
- Perfect Pose (*Siddhasana*), also known as Burmese Position
- Half-Lotus (*Ardha Padmasana*)
- Lotus Pose (*Padmasana*)

Easy Pose

Hero Pose

Perfect Pose

Half Lotus

Lotus Pose

It's also fine to sit on a stool, in a straight-backed chair, or an ergonomic chair (with your pelvis cast forward and feet tucked under). If on a straight-backed chair, you can scoot forward to the edge of the chair, so that your spine is extending upward, free from contact with the back of the chair. Alternatively, you can use pillows for padding between your back and the back of the chair. In either case, place your feet flat on the floor, hip distance apart and directly beneath your knees.

If, for whatever reason, sitting is not an option for you, feel free to stand or to lie down during your meditation practice. What's most important is to choose a posture in which your whole body can feel relaxed. Sitting is a good choice for beginners, because an upright spine supports mental alertness. But it's possible to practice meditation in any position at all. Find what works for you.

Settling In

The initial settling-in process is the same, whether you're sitting directly on the floor, on a cushion, meditation bench, or chair:

1. **Release tension.** Take a couple of deep, slow breaths. As you exhale, release any tension in your face, neck, jaw, or shoulders. Imagine saying "ahh" to help release the jaw. Smile gently to help release tension in the tiny muscles of the face. Let your skull float happily, like a helium balloon, right on top of your spine.

2. **Tongue to upper palate.** If you'd like, you can float the tip of your tongue up to gently touch the roof of your mouth, right behind the upper front teeth. Experiment to see if this feels comfortable. If it feels better to just let your tongue rest in the bottom of your mouth, that's fine too.

3. **Attention to *hara*.** Now drop your attention into the space of your lower abdomen, below the navel. This space is known as the *hara* (Japanese) or *dantian* (Chinese). It's a field of subtle energy that will help you feel grounded and stable in your meditation practice. Shine the light of your awareness gently into this space. For several rounds of inhaling and exhaling, imagine your breath emerging from this space and returning to it.

4. **Roots and trunk.** Feel the support of the floor, cushion, bench, or chair beneath you. Receive this support fully. Now imagine that you're a tree, sending roots deeper and deeper into the earth. Feel your "sitting bones" (the bones beneath the flesh of your butt)—or the soles of your feet, if you're sitting on a chair—becoming heavy, releasing, and then gently extending downward. Feel your spine, like the trunk of a tree, growing upward as your sitting bones descend.

> 66
>
> *Who you really are, on the most basic level, in your own direct experience, is simple present-moment awareness. And the essential true nature of this awareness is itself happiness, peace and pure bliss.*
>
> —Francis Bennett, *I Am That I Am*

MEDITATION

Letting Go of Thoughts

In this meditation, you'll be cultivating what's sometimes referred to as the "witness consciousness" or the "energy of mindfulness." It's the part of you that is able simply to observe thoughts and internal images as they arise and dissolve without getting caught in them.

Think of the thoughts and images as waves on the surface of an ocean—and the part of you that observes them as the deepest part of the ocean. Even in the midst of a raging storm—with towering waves crashing and churning—the depths remain calm, still, and silent.

You might also think of the images and thoughts as the characters in a movie, and your awareness of them as the theater screen upon which they appear. Does the screen get emotionally involved in the plot of the movie? Does the screen have an intellectual or political agenda? Does the screen get infatuated with certain characters and hate others? No, the screen is an absolutely neutral witness, while at the same time being the true substance of the characters, and hence infinitely intimate with them.

And now set your timer for five minutes, ten minutes, or longer, and press start. Place the timer next to you. Settle in, using the instructions on page 58.

1. **Notice the contents of the mind.** Turn your attention inward, and begin noticing the contents of your mind: the internal chatter, or mental dialogue, as well as the images on your internal screen.

2. **Label thoughts, images, and rest.** In this practice, you'll be using three labels. Each time you notice a thought, label that thought as "talk." (State the label internally to yourself, in a friendly, kind, and matter-of-fact voice.) Each time you notice an internal image (a picture in your mind), label that image as "image." When neither thought nor image is present, label that stillness or gap in mind activity as "rest." As you label the thoughts and images, maintain the attitude of a detached but kind observer, almost as though you are saying, "Hello, thoughts," or "Hello, images," in a friendly and relaxed way. Make no attempt to change the thoughts or images. Simply observe and label them with this attitude of benevolent indifference. On their own, they will arise, abide for a certain amount of time, and then dissolve. Remember: If you get distracted, just notice that this has happened, enjoy the "magic moment," and bring yourself gently back to the practice.

3. **Notice awareness itself.** Now turn your attention toward the part of you that is noticing and labeling the thoughts, images, and stillness or gaps. In other words, shine the light of awareness on awareness itself. Try to get a sense of who or what it is that's actually *doing* the noticing. This is the part of your mind that remains forever untouched by its contents, or by the thoughts and images arising within it. Explore these questions: Does this awareness have limits? Does it have a boundary? Can you locate its edges and step beyond them? Is there a difference between the awareness that is being observed, right now, and the awareness that's doing the observing?

4. **Notice how you feel.** When your timer goes off, take a couple of deep, slow breaths, and take note of any feelings or sensations that may have arisen.

> 66
>
> *We should never forget: What we are looking for is what is looking.*
>
> —Wei Wu Wei, *Posthumous Pieces*

How did that go? Were you able to tune in to the contents of your mind and apply the labels? Did you notice that the contents of your mind (the thoughts and images) are in constant motion? This is an insight into impermanence of phenomena, which might feel a bit unsettling, but can also be hugely empowering. Because things are constantly changing, it's futile to hold on to them, to expect them to remain unchanging. On the other hand, it's precisely because things are changing that transformation and healing are possible.

What did you discover about awareness itself? Is it limited in any way? Is it bound by space or time? Does it come and go in the way that thoughts and images do? What are its inherent qualities?

These are all very interesting questions to explore, so let yourself be curious about them. Don't worry too much about getting specific answers. These will arrive—some verbally, some intuitively—in their own time. Just give the questions space to dance within your heart and mind. Let them draw you into their mystery and reveal their clarity when they (and you) are ready. There's no hurry.

Perhaps you also noticed that the thoughts and images about yourself (that is, your self-image) are also continuously transforming. This is another intriguing insight into impermanence. Your self-image, like all other images, is open to continuous revision, creative enhancement, or complete dissolution. It's the "me" character in your movie. Just remember: The screen of awareness is the true actor, who just happens now to be appearing in this role.

—— TAKE TEN ——

Dealing with Performance Anxiety

You've worked for 10 years as a tax accountant. You love what you do and have become quite good at it. Recently you were invited to speak at the annual meeting of the National Society of Accountants. You feel honored and excited to present your work to such an esteemed gathering of your colleagues.

Yet now, in your hotel room, just hours before you'll be taking the stage, the excitement has been fully upstaged by abject terror. A train of worst-case scenarios hurtles through your mind: *What if my computer crashes and takes my PowerPoint images with it? What if a challenging question makes me look foolish?*

This is the perfect moment to practice the Letting Go of Thoughts meditation. So, find a place to sit. Take a couple of deep, slow breaths. Smile gently and say "ahh" to relax your jaw completely. Now turn your attention inward to the stream of thoughts and images—the hopes, concerns, and worst-case scenarios—arising in your mind. Just watch as though you were at the movies, taking in a drama, comedy, or action flick. Label and let go (as per the instructions).

When you open your eyes, take a moment to glance around the hotel room, noticing shapes and colors. Notice how you feel. Can you tune in to a sense of ease internally? Can you again confidently enjoy the energy of excitement? Understand that an audience of people can, just like the lamps and table in your hotel room, be perceived as simply shape, color, and sound—and the silent space between.

Success is guaranteed. Imagine a being made completely of salt who decides to go for a swim in the ocean in search of salt and ends up dissolving completely—and then playfully reforms, filled with joy over its discovery. Meditation is similar: What we're looking for is already who we are. Meditation, like a swim in the ocean, helps us to realize this. What dissolves is the idea that we are separate from the ocean. What we come to understand is that the ocean is within us, always. That's all there is to it.

> 66
>
> *All thoughts, perceptions, and sensations appear in silence. We have to be open for this silence, this Presence, to be limitless, to be infinite, to be an utterly different dimension—to be just one Presence, aware in each of us and in all sentient beings. Open to the possibility that this same Presence creates a unique universe from the vantage point of each being, so that we can enjoy this extraordinary video game of life, which is so beautifully interactive that we have these tools called bodies in order to play the game from the inside.*
>
> —Francis Lucille, unpublished transcript
> (www.francis.lucille.com)

MEDITATION

Using a Mantra

A mantra is a sound, word, or phrase that's gently repeated, either out loud or silently. The sound becomes a support for meditation—a resting place for the mind, a safe harbor. The sound of the mantra interrupts the stream of monkey-mind thinking, creating gaps through which you're able to flow into deeper levels of your being. Eventually, attention comes to rest in the silence out of which the mantra emerges.

Any sound, word, or phrase can be used as a mantra. What tends to be most useful is to choose either a word/phrase that feels inspiring to you or a sound that has no conceptual meaning. An inspiring word/phrase might be something like *all is well* or *peace*. Or it could be the name of a deity, saint, or sage with whom you resonate. A sound with no conceptual meaning might be one of the seed syllables of the *chakras* (energy centers within the subtle, or nonphysical, body) or the syllable *om*, which is considered by some to be the origin of all sound.

So now, choose a word or phrase or syllable that you find inspiring. If nothing comes to mind, use *om*. Set your timer for five minutes, ten minutes, or longer, and press start. Place the timer next to you. Settle in, using the instructions on page 58.

1. **Repeat the mantra out loud.** In a gentle and pleasant voice (as though singing a lullaby to yourself), chant or speak the mantra. Keep the chanting more or less continuous, with no more than a few seconds between each round of the chanted sound, word, or phrase. If you're using a word or phrase that has an uplifting meaning, let those images and associations

naturally arise. If, for instance, you're chanting peace, enjoy the feeling of peace that slowly emerges. Whatever mantra you've chosen, become intimately aware of its quality as sound as pure vibration. Feel the sound vibrating within you, resonating within every cell of your body.

2. **Repeat the mantra in a whisper.** After repeating the mantra out loud for a while in your most resonantly beautiful voice, shift into repeating it as a whisper. Let the whispers become softer and subtler with each repetition, allowing them to transition effortlessly—even mysteriously—into an internal repetition of the mantra.

3. **Repeat the mantra internally.** As you repeat the mantra internally, completely relax your jaw, lips, tongue, and throat. At this point, it's only your mind doing the chanting. Imagine the mantra being "spoken" from deep within your heart-space.

4. **Follow sound into silence.** After repeating the mantra internally for a while, let go of the mantra completely. Rest in silence. If the mantra continues on its own, through no apparent effort on your part, that's fine. Just let it happen. Each time, follow it back into its source, which is silence. Consider the possibility that who you are, most essentially, is this silence, this source of all sound.

5. **Notice how you feel.** When your timer goes off, take a couple of deep, slow breaths, and note any feelings or sensations that may have arisen. Notice the "space" of awareness that remains as the feelings come and go.

Did you find the mantra meditation to be enjoyable and relaxing? Tedious and frustrating? A little of each? Honor and appreciate your experience, whatever it was.

Further Explorations

- Let yourself become increasingly curious about the transition between a mantra spoken out loud and a mantra spoken internally.

- Be curious about the difference between the intentional thinking of a mantra and the autopilot thinking of monkey mind. How are they different? How are they similar? In a certain sense, mantra meditation is like using a thorn to remove a thorn. You use the thorn of a mantra to uproot the much more painful and obnoxious thorn of monkey mind. Then, as you rest in silence, the "mantra thorn" itself is released.

- Notice how any word can be heard simply as a sound that is devoid of meaning. Take, for instance, the word "pizza." When you first say this word, you'll almost certainly associate it with your favorite variety of cheese and sauce on crust. But if you continue to say it over and over again, in the manner of a mantra, little by little it becomes just sound: no more inherently meaningful than *om*. What's happening is that you're letting go of a set of mental images (e.g., cheese, sauce, crust) and whatever thoughts and feelings are associated with these, and instead you're noticing that the word "pizza" is essentially just sound. And consider: Where does that sound come from? Where does it go after it's been spoken?

MEDITATION

Scanning the Body

Like many forms of meditation, body scanning is simple but not necessarily easy. As you will see, the technique itself is quite straightforward. Doing it well and fully enjoying its benefits require some practice. It's like learning how to bake croissants. The ingredient list is relatively simple: flour, water, milk, sugar, butter, yeast, and salt. None of these ingredients is exotic or difficult to find. There's no special equipment required. What is necessary is good technique, which—as any pastry chef will tell you—requires some time and effort to cultivate.

As you explore the body-scanning technique, know that you're moving step by step in the direction of a delicious outcome. Celebrate the fact that, in no time at all, you'll be enjoying the delicate fragrance of something even more satisfying than a croissant.

And now set your timer for 10 minutes or longer, and press start. Place the timer next to you. Settle in, using the instructions on page 58.

1. **Internally scan your body from top to bottom and from bottom to top.** In this practice, you're going to use your mind to internally scan the territory of your body. To begin, place your attention at the crown of your head. Let the attention remain there for three to five seconds, simply taking note of any sensations that arise. Then scan your face in a similar fashion, followed by the back and sides of your head. Continue the scan in the neck and throat area. Then your right arm, from shoulder to hand and back to shoulder. Then your left arm, from shoulder to hand and back to shoulder. Continue like this, scanning every part of your body all the way down to

your toes. When you've completed the trip from top to bottom, reverse the order. Scan your body from your toes all the way back up to the crown of your head.

The idea is to become intimately aware of the sensations in the various parts of your body without the addition of verbal commentary. If you notice you've added a judgment ("I hate that feeling" or "What an excellent sensation") or an explanation ("My elbow hurts because I played tennis for seven hours yesterday"), acknowledge these thoughts in the spirit of a "magic moment" and then return to noticing just the sensation itself.

2. **Repeat.** Continue this internal scanning process, casting the light of your attention, the light of your awareness—with an attitude of benevolent indifference—upon each and every part of your body. Move at a rate that allows you to complete about one full scan (top to bottom and back to top) in about eight minutes. (This translates to about eight full scans per hour.)

3. **Feel your body as a balloon.** Once you've become comfortable with the basic body-scanning technique, you can play with this next step. Imagine that your body is hollow like a balloon, and really feel the sensation. Sense the subtle life-force energy circulating freely within the space of your "body-balloon," like a gentle breeze in an open room. Imagine that this subtle energy rides on the breath. Now let the walls of the room—the skin of the balloon—dissolve. Feel the energy-infused space within your body become one with the energy-infused space outside of your body.

4. **Notice how you feel.** When your timer goes off, take a couple of deep, slow breaths, and take note of any feelings or sensations that may have arisen. Notice also the awareness that remains, even as the sensations come and go.

Tips and Suggestions

- Maintain your stance as a neutral observer. Avoid the temptation to consider one sensation more or less important than another.

- If certain areas of your body feel numb or fuzzy, just note the numbness or fuzziness as a sensation. As the practice deepens, more subtle levels of sensation will come to the fore. Trust that you're noticing exactly what you need to be noticing right now and the layers will peel away naturally in due time.

- Notice that the sensations come and go. Like a flowing river, bodily sensations are ever-changing. Seeing this clearly is insight into their impermanence.

- Avoid the temptation to jump from one place in your body to another. Stay with the general pattern of moving from crown to toes and back again. It will, of course, be a little different each and every time, and you can let yourself explore in new ways. But don't be magnetized by particularly strong (pleasant or unpleasant) sensations, enticing you to leap into their territory. Cultivate equanimity, and maintain your dedication to flowing through the scan calmly and progressively.

✳ *You are the light of awareness. No matter how many years, decades, or eons a cave has remained in darkness, the moment a lamp is lit, the darkness is dispelled. Similarly, the darkness of confusion, anxiety, and frustration can be transformed within the light of your awareness (the very awareness that is aware of the words on this page right now). Meditation practice invites the return, again and again, to this brightness: the flame of awareness.*

————— TAKE TEN —————

Disentangling Pain and Suffering

The experience of physical pain comes with having a human body. And it serves a very useful purpose. Pain is like a red light flashing on the dashboard of your car. It lets you know that something's not quite right and an adjustment is required. If you've brushed up against a hot stove, pain shouts, "Move!" So pain itself is not a problem. What makes the situation seem unbearable is not the physical pain itself, but rather the mental-emotional overlays: the stories you tell yourself about the pain.

Say you've been meditating in what you thought was your most comfortable position, but your legs are killing you. Your knees are throbbing. You begin to wonder, *Will this ridiculous practice render me disabled?* You feel a mounting agitation. Your mind races into fantasy: a hot bath—no, a deep-tissue massage. The feeling of irritation returns, along with another cramp. You curse softly under your breath.

This is a perfect moment to apply a variation of the body-scanning technique. Here's how: As you scan, notice emotional feelings (e.g., anger, sadness, fear, etc.) along with the physical sensations. Apply the label "feel" to each emotional feeling and apply the label "touch" to each physical sensation. So, for instance, if you notice a burning sensation, say to yourself, "Touch." If you observe a feeling of sadness, say to yourself, "Feel." As you disentangle physical sensation from emotional reactions, the quality of the sensation is likely to transform—becoming more spacious, more fluid, and perhaps less painful.

MEDITATION

Focusing on a Candle Flame

Gently focusing your gaze on the flame of a candle is a beautiful way to cultivate concentration and help the mind settle into calmness and tranquility. For meditation purposes, choose an unscented, simple candle to avoid adding distraction. In other words, leave the rainbow-striped, 16-inch, rose-scented wax-candle bust of Johnny Depp for a social occasion. A simple pure beeswax candle is perfect for this meditation.

Place the candle on a flat surface at a height that allows its flame to be directly at eye level. You should be able to gaze easily at the flame without twisting or craning your neck. Comfort is key. Clear away any other objects occupying the space around the candle, so it stands on its own. Close the windows, turn off the fan, and eliminate any other source of air turbulence, so the flame can be relatively stable and quiet.

And now, without further ado, set your timer for five minutes, ten minutes, or longer, and press start. Place the timer next to you. Light the candle and settle in, using the instructions on page 58.

1. **Rest your attention on the flame.** Let your gaze rest gently on the flame in a relaxed yet continuous way. Avoid pinching or straining your forehead or squinting your eyes. Instead, allow your eyes to soften, relaxing more deeply back into their sockets. Release your jaw, feeling a sense of spaciousness inside your mouth. Allow your gaze to be receptive, as if you're inviting the image of the flame into your eyes rather than reaching out to grab it.

2. **Keep coming back.** If you find your eyes darting around the room, no problem (it's the "magic moment"); just bring yourself back to the flame. If you find yourself being drawn into an internal movie of some sort (planning, memory, fantasy), no problem; just bring yourself back to the flame.

3. **Be interested; fall in love.** Notice the beauty of the flame. Notice its colors, its subtle movements, and its dance above the pool of melted wax. Feel its purity, its stillness, its light. Be amazed by your good fortune to have met such a friend. Fall in love. Feel satisfied, content beyond measure.

4. **Notice how you feel.** When your timer goes off, take a couple of deep, slow breaths, and take note of any feelings or sensations that may have arisen. Rest for a moment as the space of awareness within which these feelings appears and disappears.

Variations

- Instead of using a candle, use a single stem of your favorite flower, such as a rose, iris, or orchid. Everything else about the exercise is the same: receptive gaze, keep coming back, be interested, fall in love, and notice how you feel.

- As you gaze at the flame of the candle, keep yourself from blinking until your eyes begin to water. Then close your eyes and focus on the flame's afterimage, which will appear like the negative of a photograph behind your closed eyes. In a relaxed way, hold this afterimage for as long as you can. Then open your eyes, and repeat the process once or twice.

———————————

"Drink your tea slowly and reverently, as if it is the axis on which the world earth revolves—slowly, evenly, without rushing toward the future. Live the actual moment. Only this moment is life.

—Thich Nhat Hanh, *The Miracle of Mindfulness*

CHAPTER FIVE

Movement Meditation

It's now time to apply the basic principles of meditation, which you've explored in chapter 4, to activities in which your physical body is moving. Movement meditation includes physical practices designed specifically to open, align, and clarify the subtle energy of the body.

Included in this category are body-mind disciplines such as qigong, hatha yoga, and tai chi. The body's subtle life-force energy is related to the mind in a manner similar to the relationship between a horse and its rider. The rider affects the horse even as the horse affects the rider. Just so, the mind affects subtle energy even as the body's subtle energy affects mind. Transforming the subtle body through physical practices also tends to transform mental-emotional patterns, opening the way to deeper insights. When this happens, these activities become forms of meditation.

A Beautiful Adjunct to a Sitting Practice

You can learn to approach the tasks and chores of daily life—those things you typically resist or complete mostly on autopilot—in a whole new way. These activities can become doorways into presence: vehicles for becoming more fully alive and more creatively engaged in the moment. Does this sound too good to be true? Could sweeping the floor or cutting carrots really become your daily meditation practice? It's for you to discover.

Movement meditation is a great way to keep your physical body healthy. Even 10 minutes of movement a day can, over time, create profound benefits. And learning to apply mindfulness to cooking, cleaning, picking up the kids from school, balancing your checkbook, arranging flowers, and splitting firewood is a beautiful way to integrate the insights and energy of meditation seamlessly into all aspects of your life. Little by little, your thoughts, words, and actions become expressions of wisdom, love, beauty, and compassion. This is wonderful.

The only potential downside of movement meditation is if it's used to avoid sitting practice. The French mathematician, physicist, and philosopher Blaise Pascal once said, "All of man's difficulties are caused by his inability to sit, quietly, in a room by himself." This is an observation echoed by many of the world's revered meditation teachers.

Learning to sit quietly and turn attention inward is the heart of meditation. Once the heart is healthy, it can, with joy and vigor, pump blood throughout the body, infusing every cell with "heart-essence." But to expect this sort of circulation to issue forth from a weak and unhealthy heart is unreasonable. To say, "Every activity of my life is already meditation, and therefore I don't need to practice sitting meditation," before you've even tried sitting practice is equally unreasonable.

So, yes, definitely include movement meditation in your routine and fully enjoy these explorations. But let it be balanced by a healthy dose of sitting practice, at least in the beginning.

MEDITATION

Walking with Mindfulness

Walking meditation is a wonderful way of transforming something you do every day into a deeply nourishing and enjoyable support for meditation. When you practice walking meditation, each step of your journey becomes the destination; each becomes peace and joy. Thich Nhat Hanh's book *The Long Road Turns to Joy: A Guide to Walking Meditation* is an excellent resource for more detailed instructions and thought-provoking insight from a true master of the art.

Walking meditation can be practiced on its own, at a pace that is leisurely, more rapid, or in super-slow motion. It's also nice to alternate periods of walking and sitting meditation: e.g., sit for 10 minutes, then enjoy 10 minutes of walking meditation, and then sit for another 10 minutes. Once you become familiar with this practice, you'll have a hugely versatile tool in your contemplative toolbox. The possibilities are nearly limitless: walking through a park, through the airport, from your desk to the water cooler, along the beach, to the bathroom first thing in the morning, on the Appalachian Trail.

Now set your timer for five minutes, ten minutes, or longer, and press start. Place the timer in your pocket. The settling-in process begins with step 1.

1. **Be upright, breathe deeply, release tension.** Stand with your spine upright and your shoulders relaxed, letting your arms hang naturally by your sides. Take a couple of long, slow, deep breaths. As you exhale, let go of any unnecessary tension,

smile gently, and let your attention flow deeply into your belly, hips, legs, and feet. Relax your pelvis, as if you have just mounted a horse. Feel your connection to the earth.

2. **Coordinate your breath with your steps.** Now begin to coordinate your breathing with taking small steps. As you inhale, step forward with your left foot; as you exhale, step forward with your right foot. Continue inhaling and exhaling in this manner as you move forward, while focusing your gaze gently on the ground in front of you.

3. **Kissing the earth.** As you become comfortable coordinating your breath with your steps, try adding this beautiful visualization: Each time you place one of your feet down, imagine that you are kissing the earth through the sole of your foot. Each time you pick up one of your feet, imagine that a beautiful pink and white lotus instantly blossoms in the place your foot just was. In this way, your walking becomes a way of expressing your love for the earth and of creating beauty with each step.

4. **Enjoying each step.** Walk this way—slowly, enjoying each step, with no thought of "getting somewhere" other than right where you are, here and now—until your timer indicates that time is up. Notice how you feel.

Variation

■   In step 2, experiment with taking several steps with each inhalation and several with each exhalation. But keep the pace quite slow (slower than your habitual pace) and delightfully relaxed.

Tips and Suggestions

- When the weather is nice, practicing outside is a beautiful way to receive the blessings (the energetic and aesthetic nourishment) of trees and sky.

- It's good to either go barefoot or wear shoes that give your feet and toes plenty of room to spread out. When you stretch out your feet and toes completely, the nerves, arteries, and meridians connected to the entire body are stimulated, which is very beneficial for your health.

- Let your mind be gently focused and relaxed. If it wanders into thoughts of past or future, no problem (it's the "magic moment"). Simply come back to the practice.

MEDITATIONS

Eating Mindfully

Applying mindfulness to eating begins with a basic fact: the human body requires food. Miraculous exceptions aside, a body deprived of food and water withers and dies, like a dry leaf dropping from its branch.

But our needs for nourishment go beyond the body's need for fuel. What makes a meal most nourishing, ultimately, is the *quality of energy and attention* that you bring to it. A pleasant atmosphere, an attitude of appreciation, sweet connections with friends or family members—these ingredients are equally, if not more, important to your overall health and happiness than is the nutritional makeup of the food, per se. So light a candle. Place a vase of fresh flowers on your table. Invite a new or longtime friend to join you for the meal.

What Am I Really Hungry For?

Take out a piece of paper or open a word processing file. Again and again, finish the sentence that begins, "What I'm really hungry for is . . ." Give the word "hungry" free rein to mean whatever it wants to mean. And let the "I" toggle effortlessly between I-the-body, I-the-mind, I-the-heart, and I-awareness.

Maybe you're hungry for a cheese enchilada. Maybe you're hungry for a career change or a Caribbean cruise. Maybe you're hungry for true love. Keep your pen (or typing fingers) moving for at least 10 minutes, exploring: "What I'm really hungry for is . . ."

Mindful Eating Meditation #1:
Which Is Bigger, the Universe or a Pea?

1. **Notice shape, color, scent, and texture.** Take a moment before you begin eating to contemplate the food on your plate. First become aware of its various shapes and colors. Notice the different textures. Notice your mouth watering as you see and smell the food you're about to consume.

2. **Address by name and trace genealogy.** Now take a moment to acknowledge each food by name, such as: squash, peas, tempeh, and millet. Choose one of the foods, say the peas, to explore a bit more deeply. In the manner of constructing a genealogy, bring to mind all the pea's relatives: the pea plant growing in a field, the minerals in the soil, the rain and the clouds, the bees pollinating its flowers. And then go even farther back: to the ocean that was the source of the cloud; the mountain whose runoff deposited the minerals in the soil; the people who, three hundred years ago, first cleared and plowed the field. As you'll soon discover, there's no part of the universe that isn't in some way related to this humble pea sitting on your plate.

3. **Be amazed; feel gratitude.** Each bite is the universe. The pea contains the entire universe. The entire universe is conspiring to nourish your human body. *Amazing!*

Mindful Eating Meditation #2: Feeding the Deities

1. **Envision a body of deities.** The human body contains about 100 trillion cells. Before you take your first bite of food, imagine that each of these 100 trillion cells is home to a deity: a god or goddess or archangel, a *deva* (Sanskrit for deity) or saint or sage, or whatever other inspiring entity you'd care

to imagine. Take a couple of minutes to really see and feel in your mind's eye these beings in all their glorious detail, dancing ecstatically or peacefully ruminating in their simple cell or luxurious palace.

2. **Feed the deities.** As you take a bite of food, chew and swallow, imagine that what you're actually doing is feeding the deities. You're sending them tiny packages of all their favorite foods: what's most delicious, most nourishing, and most beneficial. Like a parent sending care packages to their kids at college, you're now offering a full array of delicacies to the radiantly winged and unconditionally loving archangels. You're feeding the sublimely beautiful and endlessly playful *devas*. You're feeding the infinitely wise saints and sages. See them gratefully receiving these gifts of deep nourishment.

3. **Take delight.** What an honor and pleasure it is to have an opportunity to offer the gift of nourishment to such an esteemed retinue. Know that these deities are symbolic representations of aspects of yourself. Keep this in mind as you continue to partake in your meal, gratefully receiving your gifts.

> 66
>
> *To see a World in a Grain of Sand*
> *And a Heaven in a Wild Flower,*
> *Hold Infinity in the palm of your hand*
> *And Eternity in an hour.*
>
> —William Blake, "Auguries of Innocence"

Relating to Cravings

It's always the German chocolate cake that gets you: that luscious caramelized coconut, those tender pecans. So you say, "Just one piece." Then, feeling just a tad guilty, you take the first bite. It's delicious—and for just a moment, you actually savor it deeply. But then it's a rush to the finish line. "Just one piece" becomes two, then three, inhaled more than tasted. Now you feel saturated and, in a strange way, satisfied—but also rather sick.

Next time you feel the pull of a craving, consider tracing the genealogy of the cake and feeding the deities: Gaze for a moment at a piece of cake (placed lovingly on a beautiful plate). Notice its color, texture, and fragrance. Consider what you know about the origin of its ingredients: flour from fields of wheat, golden in the autumn sun. Eggs from chickens, wandering a farmyard or squeezed into cages. Sugar from sugarcane, from South Asia. Wow! There's a lot going on in this humble piece of cake. Be amazed. Feel grateful.

Now take a full bite of the cake. Chew it slowly, noticing how its flavor transforms as it mixes more completely with your saliva. As you swallow, imagine sending it as a gift to the deities in the cells of your body. Notice how you feel. Paying close attention to the feelings and sensations associated with a craving will, over time, allow it to lessen. Now sit quietly for a few minutes. Notice the movement of your breath. Find a depth and rhythm of inhaling and exhaling that feels most deeply satisfying. Smile gently, knowing (once again) that you fully deserve all that's most truly nourishing.

Hatha Yoga as a Form of Movement Meditation

Perhaps you already practice yoga. If so, you've likely discovered some of its physical benefits: relaxation, strength, flexibility, balance, and increased energy. What you may not know is that yoga can also be a wonderful tool for cultivating the energy of mindfulness. Just 10 minutes, first thing in the morning, beautifully wakes up your body and mind. Just 10 minutes at midday can provide a welcome cure for tight shoulders, along with an easy attitude adjustment.

The meaning of the Sanskrit word "yoga" is "union with the infinite" or "union with the divine." Yoga comes in a variety of types, all of which were originally intended to be forms of meditation. This is true also of hatha yoga—the kind involving physical poses (*asanas*) and movements. Here are some tips on how to cultivate the energy of mindfulness via your yoga *asana* practice:

- Always begin your practice by taking a couple of minutes to tune in to your breath. Feel your abdomen gently rising and falling, as the breath flows into and out of your body. Then, as you begin to move through the various yoga poses, remain gently aware of the breath. Feel that the breath is leading the movements, that the poses are blossoming out of the ground of the breath.

- Cultivate an open-minded and exploratory approach to your *asana* practice. Notice physical sensations arising and dissolving. Be aware of sensations of flowing energy (known as *prana* or *qi*). Notice also the arising and dissolving of thoughts and emotions; these also are part of the practice. Let the physical sensations, as well as the thoughts and emotions, arise and dissolve like clouds passing through the sky of your awareness.

- When practicing the series of poses known as the Sun Salutation (described and illustrated in the Appendix), use this as an opportunity to offer praise and gratitude to the sun. Without the sun, life on earth (at least as we now know it) would be impossible. There would be no photosynthesis and hence no trees or flowers. It would be dark and really cold. There would be no beautiful sunsets or sunrises. Acknowledging the sun's pivotal role in your survival as a human being, you salute the sun.

At the same time, but on a deeper level, offer salutations of praise and gratitude to the *sun of awareness* within you. You can imagine this sun of awareness to be localized in your heart-space, though in reality it has no space-time location. It's the source of space and time and of all the phenomena—trees and flowers and humans alike—dancing upon the space-time stage. It's looking through your eyes right now.

- Practice loving-kindness, compassion, and respect in relation to your physical body. If you notice yourself becoming overly aggressive, relax into a more spacious and gentle enthusiasm.

> 66
>
> *It's simple to listen quietly, yet it's not easy, because there is a tremendous momentum of habit to create stimulation through fantasy. This is particularly noticeable when we're removed from our daily life during retreat, when we are without our accustomed morning-till-night stimulation—no excitement through the media, through relationships, work, noise, music, entertainment, movies.*
>
> —Toni Packer, *The Light of Discovery*

- Be open to the possibility that your body may be something other than what you think it is, and that you also may be something other than what you think yourself to be.

- Always end your practice with Corpse Pose (*Shavasana*).

Virtually Any Physical Activity Can Support Your Meditation Practice

While yoga, qigong, and tai chi are designed specifically to support meditation, other physical activities can easily be approached in a contemplative way, such as walking (see page 77), hiking, horseback riding, running, golf, and tennis. Basketball coach Phil Jackson became famous for his incorporation of meditation techniques into his team's training regimen. Honestly, any physical activity can be a support for mindfulness. How? By being fully aware of the movements as you're making them. By giving yourself so completely to the activity that at some point there's no longer a "you" who is "doing" the activity—but rather the activity is doing you.

Using *Gathas* in Daily Activities

To be mindful means to shine the light of awareness upon a thought, feeling, sensation, or perception, in order to see the phenomenon clearly and understand it deeply.

Mindfulness tends to flow naturally when you're genuinely interested in what you're doing. For example, a physicist who is passionate about Einstein's special theory of relativity is able, quite effortlessly, to spend long hours contemplating intricate mathematical formulas. A poet enthralled with the art of writing sonnets can with great ease maintain their current of mindfulness when considering the specifics of a poem's rhythm and tone. An athlete who is "in the zone"—whose actions are so effortlessly focused and efficient as to seem almost supernatural—is also displaying a profound level of mindfulness. They are in love with the game, and this love makes focused attention natural and easy. And when you're listening to music that you find inspiring, your enthusiasm for the music translates naturally into mindfulness. Whether it's a Mozart piano concerto or Coltrane's *A Love Supreme*, you have no problem remaining focused on the sound of the music.

In general, then, a good way to nourish mindfulness is to stay connected with the current of your interest and enthusiasm. As Joseph Campbell wisely counseled: "Follow your bliss!" But what about the more mundane daily tasks, which often leave you feeling bored or annoyed—things like taking the trash out or doing the dishes? What about daily routines: showering, brushing your teeth, or driving to work? What about activities that tend to suck you into frenetic intensity (your job on the floor of the stock exchange) or a monotonous zone of forgetfulness (surfing the Internet)?

For these sorts of activities, a *gatha* can be very useful. A *gatha* is a short practice poem whose job it is to bring you back to mindfulness. Beneath the magical touch of a *gatha*, seemingly ordinary objects and events can display great beauty and wisdom. Here are some examples, compliments of Thich Nhat Hanh:

Throwing out the Garbage. *In the garbage, I see a rose. In the rose, I see compost. Everything is in transformation. Impermanence is life.*

Turning on the Water. *Water comes from high mountain sources. Water runs deep in the Earth. Miraculously, water comes to us and sustains all life. My gratitude is filled to the brim.*

Using the Telephone. *Words can travel thousands of miles. May my words create mutual understanding and love. May they be as beautiful as gems, as lovely as flowers.*

Drinking Tea. *This cup of tea in my two hands, mindfulness held perfectly. My mind and body dwell in the very here and now.*

—— TAKE TEN ——

Taking Care of Household Chores

You still don't believe it's your turn to clean the bathroom. Even after your housemate presented the note in her date book, showing that her last week's schedule included "clean bathroom", you still don't believe it. Nevertheless, here you are, toilet brush in hand. Grumbling, you squirt some cleaner into the bowl. Resigned, you think, *Let's just get this over with, as quickly as possible.*

This is a perfect moment to apply a *gatha*. One possibility is to use Thich Nhat Hanh's practice poem for this much-maligned activity: "How wonderful to scrub and clean. Day by day, my heart and mind grow clearer."

Before you pick up the toilet brush, read the *gatha*—either out loud or silently to yourself. Read it again, and perhaps even a third time. Take a moment to consider its meaning—not in the sense of needing to figure it out definitively, but more in the spirit of curiosity, openness, and humor. Now, with the *gatha* in your mind, begin the task at hand. As you scrub, be on the lookout for any emotions (irritation, boredom) that may arise. Welcome them all without judgment—like clouds passing through the spacious "sky" of your awareness—and repeat the *gatha* once again.

Little by little, what you'll discover is that internal and external environments are interdependent. The qualities of your living space interact continuously with the qualities of your mind. Inside and outside mirror each other. This is an insight that can be cultivated as you engage in household chores with the support of *gathas* like this one.

Gathas are like the training wheels on a bicycle. When you're first learning how to ride a bicycle, training wheels can be really helpful. Each time you lose your balance—tipping to the right or to the left—the training wheels are there to bring you back to center. Once you've become skilled at maintaining your balance, the training wheels can be taken off. And before you know it, you're surfing the streets of San Francisco, joyously mounted on your Fuji Absolute road bike.

A *gatha* that is memorized or taped to your dashboard or refrigerator serves a similar purpose. If you've tipped into forgetfulness, into distraction—into the jungle of monkey mind—the *gatha* brings you back to center, to here and now, the balance point. There's no need to practice a *gatha* continuously for 10 minutes, or even for one minute. All it takes is one or two repetitions, as needed, to spark your mindfulness of the chosen activity.

It's fine to use *gathas* that are written by someone else, such as those listed earlier. It also can be fun to compose your own, if you feel so inclined. Even once you've become quite efficient at balancing on your own, these short practice poems may continue to emerge as an expression of your own creativity. Using a *gatha* is simple. Here's what you do:

1. **Choose a *gatha*.** Decide which activity you'd like to bring more mindfulness to. Find (or compose) a *gatha* that pertains to this activity.

2. **Post or memorize.** Write the *gatha* on a little piece of paper, and post it somewhere conspicuous—where you're likely to see it when you're engaged in that activity. Or you can memorize the *gatha*, trusting that it will appear on your internal screen when it's needed.

3. **Apply the *gatha*.** Commit to working with the *gatha* for a certain amount of time: two days, two weeks, two months, two years. Coordinate the reading of the lines of the *gatha* with your breathing: inhale as you read the first line, exhale as you read the second line, and so on.

4. **Notice its effects.** Every now and again, evaluate the effects the *gatha* is having on you. Are your moments of distraction fewer or of lesser duration for this particular activity? Are you tuning in to the wisdom and beauty contained within the object or activity that previously you had ignored or disdained?

5. **Feel gratitude.** How excellent it is to have this tool—the practice poem—to support you on your journey.

✳ *Japanese contemplative arts are a lovely venue for cultivating mindfulness. At some point during your journey, you may wish to explore one (or more) of the following contemplative disciplines, which are designed specifically to support a deepening sensitivity to, and intimacy with, the moment-by-moment unfolding of the activity: flower arranging (ikebana); archery (kyudo), tea ceremony (chado), calligraphy (shodo), brush painting (sumi-e), poetry (haiku), martial arts (Bushido), miniature tree cultivation (bonsai), Zen rock garden (karesansui), and court dance (bugaku). There are several choices here, so don't feel as if you need to explore them all. If one piques your interest, file it away for later in your practice.*

Judge nothing, you will be happy.
Forgive everything, you will be happier.
Love everything, you will be happiest.

—Sri Chinmoy, *The Goal Is Won*

CHAPTER SIX
Meditation to Cultivate Positive Energy

Happiness is important. We all know this intuitively. To experience peace, joy, and happiness is our deepest desire. You've probably already figured this out. If you have any doubts, check it out right now. Ask yourself, "What do I most deeply desire?"

If your answer is some object, person, or situation, apply the question once again. So, for instance, if your answer is, "What I most deeply desire is to be driving a Jaguar instead of a Nissan Sentra," then ask yourself, "Why do I want to be driving a Jaguar instead of a Sentra?" And the answer will likely be, "Because I believe that I'll feel happier driving a Jaguar than I currently am while driving a Sentra."

> 66
> *During meditation a silent mind is very important, but 'silent' does not mean closed. The silent mind is an alert, awakened mind: a mind seeking the very nature of reality. Also, the joy of silent wisdom comes from your own mind and is always there. Constantly, wherever you go, you can experience the joyful wisdom energy of the silent mind.*
>
> —Lama Yeshe, *The Peaceful Stillness of the Silent Mind*

This movement toward happiness is completely natural. And meditation is a great tool for cultivating happiness in all its various flavors: as friendliness, joy, contentment, loving-kindness, compassion, peace, tenderness, playfulness, humor, spontaneity, comfort, ease, and equanimity.

Happiness as the Ground of Clear Seeing

In the context of meditation, happiness is important not only as an outcome—as a delicious fruit of the practice—but also as part of the path. Feelings of happiness and contentment are like potent fertilizer that nourishes the flowers of "clear-seeing." Tuning in to peace and happiness is like moving from the whirling outskirts to the eye of the hurricane. From that still center, you can observe the situation more clearly and objectively.

The lasting happiness accessed through meditation practice provides a sweet addition to happiness in its more temporary forms. Although the melt-in-your-mouth experience of an almond croissant is fantastic, it doesn't last more than 10 or 15 minutes. No matter how mindfully you consume the croissant, in the end it's gone completely. The happiness accessed via meditation is more like a subterranean current of joy that flows continuously. It's a thread of contentment that stitches together the garment of your moment-by-moment experience.

So let yourself fully enjoy the pleasant feelings and sensations that arise as you explore the meditations in this chapter. Let them nourish you deeply. Understand that they're a kind of medicine: mother's milk.

MEDITATION

Inner Smile

In this meditation to nourish peace and joy, you'll learn how to cultivate "smile-energy" and then direct that energy to every cell and organ of your body. As the cells and organs receive this nourishing gift of smile-energy, they themselves will begin to laugh and smile as an expression of their contentment and delight. Before you know it, your entire body will be smiling from the inside out.

Set your timer for five minutes, ten minutes, or longer. Press start. Place the timer next to you. Settle in, using the instructions on page 58.

1. **Tongue to roof of mouth.** Rest the tip of your tongue gently on the roof of your mouth, right behind your upper front teeth. You'll find the spot that feels perfect.

2. **Smile gently.** Now smile gently, allowing your lips to feel full and smooth as they spread out to the sides, and lift just slightly. Let this smile be similar to the Mona Lisa smile or how you smile to yourself when you've suddenly gotten a joke you heard several days ago.

3. **Tune in to the brow center.** Bring your attention now to the center of your forehead: the space between your eyebrows, also known as the "third eye." As you rest your attention here, subtle energy will begin to gather that is a sense of warmth or fullness. Imagine this place to be like a pool of warm water. As the energy of awareness pools here, let your attention drift deeper into that pool, back toward the center of your head, the space between your ears.

4. **Rest attention in the crystal palace.** Let your attention rest now right here in the center of your brain—in the space between the two hemispheres. This is a place that's sometimes referred to as the crystal palace. It's the home of several powerful endocrine glands: the pineal, pituitary, thalamus, and hypothalamus. Feel the energy of awareness now gathering in this powerful place.

5. **Create smiling eyes.** Allow the energy gathering in the crystal palace to flow forward now into your eyes. Imagine and feel your eyes becoming "smiling eyes." To enhance this, you can imagine that you're gazing into the eyes of the person you love the most and they're gazing back at you, infusing your eyes with this delicious quality of loving-kindness and delight.

6. **Smile to your heart.** Now direct the energy of your smiling eyes back and down into the left side of your torso to your heart. Imagine and feel that you are smiling down to your heart as it beats within your chest. With gratitude and appreciation, send the energy of a smile—the energy of loving-kindness—down into your heart. See and feel your heart receiving this gift fully: soaking up smile-energy like a sponge soaks up water. Repeat this, if you'd like, with your other internal organs: your liver, your kidneys, your lungs, your spleen or stomach, or any organ you'd like to embrace with smile-energy.

7. **Welcome the "smiling-body."** Now imagine sending smile-energy into every bone, muscle, and cell of your body. See and feel each bone, each muscle, and each cell receiving this smile-energy, drinking it in, feeling deeply nourished and fully satisfied. Now feel that your entire body has become a smiling-body. Imagine and feel your body, from head to toe, pulsing and flowing with smile-energy.

8. **Notice how you feel.** When your timer goes off, release the tip of your tongue from the roof of your mouth, and let go of the smile (or keep it, if it now feels natural). Take a couple of deep, slow breaths, and take note of any feelings or sensations that may have arisen.

Tips and Suggestions

- Though it's nice to begin with the heart, this practice can be used to smile to any bodily location: your brain, your ankle, your left little finger, whatever. Send smile-energy (in the spirit of a bouquet of flowers and a get well soon card) into places that are injured or ill. Send smile-energy into places that feel numb, as a gentle invitation to come out of hiding and join the party.

- Remember to maintain the quality of a gentle and genuine smile, infused with the energy of loving-kindness and compassion, particularly when directing your inner smile to an injured place. If you notice frustration, anger, condemnation, fear, or judgment creeping in, take a couple of deep breaths, then connect again with loving-kindness and compassion.

- Think of the smile you generate in this practice as a physical movement that has a very specific function, like a yoga pose. It's a tool for meditation, not unlike your cushion and fully extended spine.

> 66
>
> *When you give up the idea of having a concept of the world, there is no problem with dealing with reality since there is no mental formation giving you a signal that reality ought to be different from what it is.*
>
> —Daniel Odier, *Doors of Joy*

Having a Bad Day

You're having a bad day. You were late to work because the cat got out, and it took you 45 minutes to get her safely back inside. Now, having at long last arrived at your office, you realize that the big project you thought was due tomorrow is actually due at noon today.

You feel a tightening in your jaw. A swell of frustration and panic. Your breathing becomes more rapid and shallow. You struggle to hold back a brimming stream of tears.

This is the perfect moment to take a 10-minute time-out to practice the Inner Smile meditation. Close the door to your office (or find an empty room to practice in). Turn off your cell phone. Sit down. Take a couple of deep breaths, and begin cultivating the inner smile as you've learned it. The inner smile becomes smiling eyes.

Now locate the particular places in your body that are holding the "having a bad day" feelings and sensations. The panic sensation, for instance, may be hanging out primarily in the pit of your belly. The frustration may be lodged in your jaw and the sadness at the back of your throat. (It may be different for you.) As you inhale, tune in to the particular feeling or sensation in its specific bodily location. As you exhale, imagine sending a gentle stream of smile-energy into that place. Notice how you feel.

This exercise is not about getting rid of the feeling or sensation. Instead, you're creating space for the feelings and sensations to flow and transform in the most beneficial ways. Now you can more calmly go about "putting out the fire."

MEDITATION

Loving-Kindness

In the Inner Smile meditation, you learned how to send the energy of loving-kindness to every cell and organ of your body. In this meditation, you'll be doing something similar. You'll be sending the energy of loving-kindness first to yourself and then to each and every living being—to all the cells within your universal body. In this way, you'll be developing *unconditional* love and affection.

Set your timer for five minutes, ten minutes, or longer. Press start. Place the timer next to you. Settle in, using the instructions on page 58.

1. **Reflect and remember kindness received.** Take a few moments to reflect on your life. Imagine yourself moving through a typical day: going to work, preparing meals, relating to friends and family, celebrating. Reflect on your goals and aspirations— what you're passionate about and what you hope to accomplish. See that you genuinely wish to be happy, and that pretty much everything you do is for the purpose of creating happiness. And know that you are completely deserving of happiness.

    Recall a specific instance in which someone was kind to you in a way that supported your happiness. Bring up the memory of how you *felt* in that moment in as much detail as possible. Notice the sensations generated in your body as you remember this instance of kindness received.

2. **Wish yourself happiness.** Now, in the manner of a gentle mantra, repeat the following, either out loud (in a relaxed and soothing voice) or internally: *May I be safe. May I be happy. May I be healthy. May I enjoy comfort and ease.* Continue for several minutes, wishing yourself happiness. Don't be shy.

Don't be bashful. Let go of any feelings of unworthiness or awkwardness that may arise, in relation to wishing yourself happiness. You are 100 percent deserving!

3. **Reflect and remember kindness offered.** Take a few moments now to reflect upon the lives of other human beings. Since it's rather challenging to visualize the lives of 7.1 billion people, narrow it down to include only those who are closest to you: parents, children, spouse, lover, friends, and so on. On the screen of your inner eye, see these people—your loved ones—moving through their typical days. Reflect on the fact that they too (just like you) have goals and aspirations. They too want to be happy. And because you genuinely care about them, you also wish them to be happy. You know that they—just like you—are completely deserving of happiness.

    Now, recall a specific instance in which you were kind to another person in a way that supported his or her happiness. Bring up the memory of how you felt in that moment in as much detail as possible. Notice the sensations it generates in your body—to remember this instance of loving-kindness extended to another.

4. **Wish others happiness.** Now, surfing on the sweet feeling of that memory, repeat the following, either out loud or internally: *May all beings be safe. May all beings be happy. May all beings be healthy. May all beings enjoy comfort and ease.* Continue for several minutes, wishing all beings the gift of happiness, health, safety, comfort, and ease. Understand deeply that, just like you, all beings—all 7.1 billion humans, as well as all nonhuman beings—wish for and are 100 percent deserving of happiness.

    Feel a sense of tender connection with all living beings: a purely impersonal yet intimate affection, rooted in the simple understanding that, just like you, each and every being wishes to be happy. Just like you, each and every being deserves happiness. Feel the spontaneous blessing—the sense of universal benediction—that comes with this.

5.   **Rest as a cell in the universal body.** Return to the image of your human body-mind as being one cell in a universal body. Imagine your good wishes radiating outward, like a gentle ripple, to every other cell of the body.

6.   **Notice how you feel.** When your timer goes off, relax, take a couple of deep, slow breaths, and take note of any feelings or sensations that may have arisen.

Tips and Variations

- Send loving-kindness to someone specific—a friend, a coworker, your neighborhood bank teller, the homeless person on the street, the politician who you most dislike. The process is exactly the same, except that as you visualize that person, say: *May you be safe. May you be happy. May you be healthy. May you enjoy comfort and ease.*

- Play with offering stealth blessings to complete strangers: the woman in line ahead of you in the grocery store; the receptionist at the dentist's office. In the spirit of a "random act of kindness," deliver silently—on a current of heart-energy— the words: *May you be safe. May you be happy. May you be healthy. May you enjoy comfort and ease.*

- Remember, generating thoughts of loving-kindness and compassion for someone doesn't mean that you have to invite them over for tea. Everyone wishes to be happy and free from suffering. This is the truth that you tap into as fuel for the meditation. Not everyone is going to be your best friend or lover. You can wish someone well without necessarily liking them in a personal way.

Losing Touch with an Old Friend

Your old college roommate, with whom you shared so many excellent times, hasn't phoned or texted for eons. Though you were best friends for nearly 10 years, you now live in separate cities, hundreds of miles apart. You feel the impulse to reconnect, but aren't sure how to proceed.

This is a perfect moment to devote some time to a Loving-Kindness meditation. Here's how: First, allow all the images of this person (from your various memories) to emerge. Welcome any physical sensations or emotions that may also arise. Notice the storylines: your theories about why she hasn't called, what should or shouldn't have happened, etc. Once you've fully welcomed them, allow this swirl of feelings, thoughts, and images to gently recede into the background.

Now begin the Loving-Kindness meditation, directed first to yourself, then to your friend, and finally with your relationship in mind, saying, *Together may we be safe. Together may we be happy. Together may we be healthy. Together may we enjoy comfort and ease.* Repeat this practice for seven days in a row, each time generating unconditional love and affection for yourself, then for your friend, and then for your relationship. By the end of seven days, a new equanimity and clarity will likely have emerged. At that point, you'll be able to use your intuition—your direct knowing—to skillfully guide your actions.

Perhaps you'll renew the connection. Perhaps you won't. The specific outcome is less important than the process of generating the energy of loving-kindness for you both.

MEDITATION

Appreciation and Gratitude

Generating appreciation and gratitude is one of the most direct ways to create a flow of positive energy and emotion. The reason for this is simple: Appreciation and gratitude are based in feelings of connection. They're rooted in a conscious acknowledgment of relationship—of your flowing interdependence with all that is. As such, feelings of appreciation and gratitude are directly aligned with reality. They're an expression of how things actually are.

> 66
>
> *If your mind is happy then you are happy anywhere you go.*
>
> *When wisdom awakens within you, you will see Truth wherever you look.*
>
> *Truth is all there is. It's like when you learned how to read, you can then read anywhere you go.*
>
> —Ajahn Chah, *The Teachings of Ajahn Chah*

Negative thought patterns, on the other hand, tend to be based in beliefs and feelings of separation: a sense of there being an isolated "me" that's at war with a specific (my horrible boss) or general (the capitalist economy) "other." Feelings of resentment, jealousy, suspicion, aggression, arrogance, and judgment grow out of this belief of separation. They create physical, mental, and emotional constriction. They're uncomfortable. They're the symptoms of suffering.

When you're resonating with appreciation and gratitude, not only are you in alignment with the truth of interdependence—of your interconnectedness with all living beings—but you're also dialing in to intuitive and nonlocal aspects of yourself. In other words, you're opening a portal to Wisdom Mind, the part of you that transcends space and time. As the boundaries between self and other begin to soften, your connection to universal intelligence becomes more immediate and direct.

In this meditation, you'll be tuning in to the crystal palace: the space in the center of your head that was introduced in the Inner Smile meditation. This is home to the pineal gland, whose crystalline structure you'll be gently activating as you cultivate feelings of appreciation and gratitude.

Part of the power of this practice is to generate a momentum of emotional energy based on the suggested contemplations. That's why these instructions are somewhat lengthier than others. Don't let this deter you from fully experiencing each step of the meditation.

> ✱ *Create a list of all the things you're grateful for. If you're feeling stuck, you can begin with: having a book about meditation in my hands and having made it all the way to chapter 6. Yeah! Here are some other possibilities: Grateful for the ability to breathe. Grateful for flowers. Grateful for Rumi's poetry. Grateful for fresh peaches right from the tree in my backyard. Take out a piece of paper or open a word processing file. Go for 10 minutes at least, completing the sentence, "I'm grateful for…" over and over again.*

And now set your timer for five minutes, ten minutes, or longer. Press start. Place the timer next to you. Settle in, using the instructions on page 58.

1. **From the heart, send appreciation and gratitude to the earth.** Let your attention settle gently into your heart-space—the center of your chest, midway between your spine and breastbone. Feel the breath—your precious life-force energy—gently circulating here. Imagine this space filling with golden-white light, bathed in the light of your awareness. And now begin to cultivate feelings of appreciation and gratitude for your physical home: the planet earth. Consider all the grains and fruits and vegetables created by the earth to nourish and sustain your physical body. Appreciate the earth for this. Consider the lakes and rivers and oceans of the earth, the sources of necessary water. Feel grateful to the earth for providing you with the water you need to survive. Continue in this way, thinking of all the things the earth provides—all the nourishment, all the protection, all the beauty. Imagine sending a pulsing stream of appreciation and gratitude from your heart-space to the earth.

2. **Shift attention to the crystal palace.** Now simply rest your attention—in a completely relaxed and receptive way—in the center of your head, the space midway between the upper tips of your ears. Another way to arrive at this space is to tune in to the center of your forehead (the "third eye") and then allow your attention to drift back from there to the center of your head. Once you're gently focused here, simply rest. Don't try to make anything happen. Just keep your attention here, gently, in the center of your head, like a feather resting in the palm of your hand. Maintain your focus here for a minute or two.

3. **Send appreciation and gratitude to Wisdom Mind.** Just for
    a moment, extend your arms upward, and bring the palms
    of your hands together, directly above your head. Do this
    just long enough to notice how far above your head your
    hands now are. Then relax your arms. Imagine a sphere of
    golden-white light hovering above your head in the place
    where your hands were. Imagine this sphere of light to be a
    symbol of your Wisdom Mind—that aspect of yourself that
    transcends time and space.

    Imagine sending feelings of appreciation and gratitude to
    this sphere of golden-white light that is your Wisdom Mind.
    Feel gratitude for the influx of wisdom, insight, creativity,
    and inspiration that flows from Wisdom Mind. Appreciate
    the power of Wisdom Mind to provide solutions to problems
    in your life. Appreciate Wisdom Mind for being your direct
    access to divinity—your direct line to universal intelligence
    and unconditional love.

4. **Feel the connection between Wisdom Mind and the crystal
    palace.** At this point, you may be feeling a flow of energy
    downward from the sphere of light into the crystal palace, that
    space in the center of your head. It may feel something like a
    gentle rain shower, bathing you in light. If you're not feeling
    this, no problem—just imagine it. See or feel the golden-white
    sphere of light above your head, connecting with the space in
    the center of your head through this gentle cascade of light.

5. **Root Wisdom Mind and the crystal palace into the heart-
    space.** Now allow that stream of energy—that gentle, sweet
    rain of light—to flow from the crystal palace down into your
    heart-space: the space within the center of your chest. From
    the heart-space, once again send feelings of gratitude and
    appreciation to Wisdom Mind.

6. **Ground into the center of the earth.** If you're feeling comfortable simultaneously holding these three points of reference (Wisdom Mind, crystal palace, and heart-space), then add a fourth one: the center of the earth. Feel and imagine that stream of golden-white light flowing from your heart-space down along the front of your spine and then all the way into the center of the earth. Feel appreciation and gratitude for the earth and for Wisdom Mind simultaneously.

7. **Notice how you feel.** When your timer goes off, relax, take a couple of deep, slow breaths, and take note of any feelings or sensations that may have arisen.

—————— TAKE TEN ——————

Wishing for More Money

You want some things only money can buy: A remodeled kitchen. An expensive dinner at your favorite French restaurant. The clothes to wear to such an occasion. And yet it just doesn't seem to be coming together. You feel frustrated and down.

This is a perfect moment to take a couple of long, deep breaths. Let go of trying to figure out the situation in the ways you have been, and instead commit to a week of Appreciation and Gratitude practice. Here's how: Set aside 10 minutes a day to devote to cultivating gratitude as a tool for connecting to Wisdom Mind. Use the first two minutes to create a list of what you're grateful for. Use the remaining eight minutes to explore the Appreciation and Gratitude meditation as a way of accessing intuitive wisdom.

Modify the practice in this way: As you're imagining a shower of golden-white light cascading down from Wisdom Mind to the crystal palace, imagine that this shower contains golden coins representing financial abundance. Think of it as a rain of blessings, received with infinite gratitude. Repeat for seven days in a row. See what happens. Very often, Wisdom Mind has solutions that conceptual mind would never have thought of. So be open to abundance appearing in ways you never would have imagined. Be willing to be utterly surprised and delighted.

Meanwhile, understand deeply that true wealth is contentment, and that Wisdom Mind is your source of true abundance. These are already here, yours for the taking.

MEDITATION

Sympathetic Joy

When you believe that the only happiness you can enjoy is the happiness experienced by a single human body-mind (namely, the one you refer to as "me" or "mine"), then happiness is a limited commodity. When you realize that you can enjoy happiness that's arising anywhere at all, and, in fact, that there's no good reason not to do this, then the reservoir of happiness becomes boundless. At the same time, all grounds for jealousy and stingy competition collapse, along with the hollow edifice of "scarcity mentality."

You realize that, from the perspective of the universal body, the joy and happiness of any one cell contributes to the joy and happiness of the entire organism, and hence all of its other cells. Seeing this clearly is the key to the door to unlimited happiness. And here it is, in the palm of your hand.

Set your timer for five minutes, ten minutes, or longer. Press start. Place the timer next to you. Settle in, using the instructions on page 58.

> 66
>
> *When you meditate long . . . the glory of the Divine shines forth. You realize then that all along there was something tremendous within you and you did not know it.*
>
> —Paramahansa Yogananda
> (www.yogananda-srf.org)

1. **Rejoice in the accomplishments of the great teachers.** Bring to mind someone who you deeply admire for their positive contributions to the world. Rejoice in this person's accomplishments. Let yourself feel totally inspired by what they have done. Generate devotion and genuine appreciation for their awesome activities. Celebrate their goodness. Feel that you're a member of this esteemed person's family, enjoying fully the happiness created by those good deeds.

   Wish for these good deeds and the joy they create to only increase. Wish for more and more people to benefit from them. Feel the joy within your body and mind as you continue to resonate with the happiness associated with this great being.

2. **Feel happy for the happiness of all living beings.** Bring to mind examples of happiness within the lives of people you know or have heard of. Let yourself feel happy for even the smallest moments of joy they experience. Feel happy for your neighbor, who's been stuck inside with the flu but is now feeling better. Celebrate along with all the players of the World Cup championship soccer team. Feel happy for the young child taking delight in blowing bubbles in the backyard on a warm summer day. Celebrate the first word spoken by a recovering stroke patient.

   Wish also that their experience of happiness increases. Wish that they one day become free from suffering and established in causeless joy. Feel a current of delight within your body and mind as you continue to resonate with the happiness of all living beings.

3. **Notice how you feel.** When your timer goes off, relax, take a couple of deep, slow breaths, and take note of any feelings or sensations that may have arisen.

Tips and Suggestions

■   Feel free to continue this meditation for as long as you'd like.
    It can build and deepen in very sweet ways.

■   Although there's no limit to the number of people in whose
    happiness you can rejoice, it's good to begin with instances
    from the lives of those who are closest to you. Then expand it
    to include the happiness of more distant acquaintances—and
    then, finally, to all living beings. This way, your sympathetic
    joy is vast, while also grounded in your daily experience.

> 66
>
> *And if at some point waves of joy permeate your body, don't
> stop there; keep your intention with pure Presence. Let the
> ocean of joy merge with this peace. We are not interested in
> anything that comes and goes. Don't abide in things; abide in
> the sweetness of things. Don't hold onto anything. Let sweet-
> ness hold you.*
>
> —Francis Lucille, unpublished transcript
> (www.francislucille.com)

TAKE TEN

Feeling Jealous of a Rival's Success

Everyone in the department refers to you as "The Three Musketeers"—one woman and two men who entered the graduate program in biology in the same year and quickly became the best of friends. For five years now, you've been nearly inseparable, supporting each other through thick and thin and working side by side in the laboratory of one of your professors, an eminent biologist who was recently awarded a Nobel Prize. She's now been invited to present her findings at a prestigious scientific conference and is allowed to bring only one assistant. She expressed her regret that she couldn't take all three of you, but was forced to choose just one, and it wasn't you.

You feel happy for your friend, but also disappointed. You then begin, in your mind, to compare your skills with those of your friend, coming to the conclusion that you actually would have been the better choice as the professor's assistant at the conference. At this point, your disappointment begins to morph into bitterness and then into a sticky, seething jealousy. You can't believe you're feeling this way about someone who's been such a dear friend for all these years, and you begin to hate yourself for it.

This is a perfect moment to call upon the Sympathetic Joy meditation as a soothing balm for the burn of jealousy.

So, take a couple of deep, slow breaths, saying "ahh" to release the tension in your jaw. As you continue with the deep, slow breathing, welcome fully all of the thoughts, feelings, and sensations associated with this situation. Let them roar and rumble like a ferocious thunderstorm. Then allow this storm to recede into the background, even if it's still rumbling ferociously. Bring your attention instead to the first step of the Sympathetic Joy meditation: rejoicing in the accomplishment of someone who has made a wonderful contribution to the planet. Choose someone who is not immediately related to the situation that has triggered the jealousy.

When you have fully experienced step 1, bring to mind the object of your jealousy: your friend. Imagine him as a small child playing in a sandbox. Imagine him building a sandcastle in which he takes great delight. See him laughing joyfully, feeling quite proud of his creation. Let yourself share in this joy that the boy is feeling, as if you were his parent. Celebrate his discovery, his playfulness, the innocent delight.

Repeat this same version of the meditation once a day for seven days. Then replace the image of the child in the sandbox with an image of your friend (at his current age) attending the conference, and continue working with the Sympathetic Joy meditation.

Do you feel a greater lightness? Were you able to connect with feelings (however fleeting) of sympathetic joy? Has the toxic energy of jealousy thinned out a bit? Can you see your work in the biology lab as a kind of play—a bit more serious, perhaps, than building sandcastles, but play nevertheless?

MEDITATION

Focus on Rest

Here's a meditation that supports relaxation. You can use it at night if you're having trouble falling asleep. You can use it during the day in the mode of a "power nap." You can use it on an airplane or on a long bus or train commute. It's a great tool for helping you tune in to the ease and peacefulness that's actually already here (but that you're not currently paying attention to), so that your body and mind can be directly and deeply nourished by it.

A good thing to understand is that deep meditation can be just as nourishing as sleep—and sometimes even more so. There's no need, then, to feel overly frustrated by not being able to doze off when you'd like to. Instead, see it as an opportunity to practice meditation, and trust that the benefits will be at least equal to those awaiting you in dreamland.

In this meditation, you'll be applying one, two, or three labels (your choice), "feeling rest," "seeing rest," or "hearing rest," as follows:

1. **Feeling rest.** As you tune in to a sense of physical relaxation in a particular place in your body or a sense of emotional peace, you'll apply the label "feeling rest."

2. **Seeing rest.** As you tune in to the blank screen of the back of your eyelids (that field of darkness that you see when you close your eyes), you'll apply the label "seeing rest."

3. **Hearing rest.** As you tune in to either internal or external silence, you'll apply the label "hearing rest." External silence means a relative absence of sound in the external environment. Internal silence means the gap between thought, when the mind is quiet.

And now set your timer for five minutes, ten minutes, or longer. Press start. Place the timer next to you. (If you're practicing this meditation at night to relax into sleep, don't use a timer.) Settle in, using the instructions on page 58.

1. **Notice places of physical relaxation.** Turn your attention inward to gently scan the terrain of your physical body. Find places that feel relaxed, and when you do, say gently to yourself, "Feeling rest." No matter how tense or stressed out you might feel, there will always be places in your body that are not tense or stressed out: your left little finger, your tongue lying in the bottom of your mouth, the back of your right knee. Notice these places, enjoy them, and acknowledge them with the label "feeling rest." Use this label to acknowledge feelings of emotional peace as well: a sense of ease, joy, or well-being, however fleeting. Appreciate these moments of emotional rest.

2. **Notice the visual rest behind your eyelids.** With your eyes closed, you can tune in to the field of darkness (or dark and light intermixed) behind your eyelids. It's like a blank movie screen, resting between the matinee and the early evening shows. It's a field of visual rest, a place without images. Each time you notice this open space behind your eyelids, apply the label "seeing rest."

3. **Notice internal and external silence.** Tune into the field of sound: external sounds as well as the sound of your own internal chatter. Now tune into the silent spaces between the sounds, or the silence that is the background of all sound. Each time you notice a moment of silence, apply the label "hearing rest."

4. **Mix and match: Continue noting and enjoying instances of rest.** Choose your favorite rest channel (e.g., feeling, seeing,

or hearing), or mix and match, noticing and labeling instances of rest along the full sensory spectrum.

5. **Notice how you feel.** When your timer goes off (or first thing in the morning before getting out of bed), relax, take a couple of deep, slow breaths, and take note of any feelings or sensations that may have arisen.

Variation

- Shorten the labels. Do you remember the mantra meditation—how you progressed from chanting the mantra out loud to whispering it and then to saying it internally and finally to allowing it to dissolve into silence? In a similar spirit, you can play with progressively shortening the labels used in this relaxation meditation: "feeling rest" can be shortened to "feel rest," and then to "rest." Once you've become familiar with noticing moments of rest, you can drop the label completely, or just use labeling occasionally as a tool to bring you back when you've become distracted.

─── TAKE TEN ───

Struggling with a Bout of Insomnia

You've tried all the tricks: counting sheep, counting backward from 100, breathing through your left nostril, humming a lullaby, applying reverse psychology and attempting to stay awake, imagining yourself lying in a flower-filled meadow. Nothing works. Your eyes are still wide open. Your body feels clenched. Your mind is racing. You desperately need to recharge—to relax and renew—before tomorrow morning's big meeting. But how?

This is a perfect moment to notice and appreciate the peace and relaxation that's already here via the Focus on Rest meditation. So, take a couple of deep, slow breaths. Close your eyes. Say "ahh" to release the tension in your jaw. Smile gently, knowing that the meditation practice is darn near close to, if not just as good as, deep sleep for charging your body-mind battery.

Follow the steps in the exercise: gently apply the label "see rest," "hear rest," or "feel rest." As you go along, see if you can infuse your meditation with a sense of curiosity and appreciation—like someone walking through a forest or jungle in search of beautiful butterflies. A butterfly with its colorful wings lands on a quivering leaf, where it is observed (with a quiet sense of awe) by the appreciative explorer. Each moment of rest is a butterfly—quiet wings shimmering with translucent color. Sweet dreams!

The moon reflected
In a mind clear
As still water:
Even the waves, breaking,
Are reflecting its light.

—Dogen, *The Zen Poetry of Dogen*

CHAPTER SEVEN

Meditation for Difficult Thoughts and Feelings

Sitting practices such as following the breath or observing thoughts create a ground of calm and clarity. Moving meditations anchor the insights of sitting practice into the physical body. Meditations to cultivate positive energy do just that: nourish and support a joyful and uplifted mind.

From this spacious and joyfully stable base, it becomes quite natural to look suffering straight in the eye: to see it clearly and embrace it tenderly. In other words, compassion arises naturally out of clarity. An agile and awake mind goes hand in hand with a tender heart, ripe with compassion.

Exploring the Practice

As you explore the practices in this chapter, keep in mind the following three tips, which will help you along your journey of learning to relate to difficult thoughts and feelings:

1. Compassion starts at home.

Remember to include yourself among the living beings you're generating compassion for. Love yourself. Appreciate yourself. Embrace yourself with the energy of tender friendliness and compassion when you notice that you're suffering. Then, little by little, you can expand this notion of "self" to include others: one other, a few others, and eventually all others. It starts, and ends, at home.

2. Don't mistake suffering for compassion.

Having compassion for someone doesn't mean being drawn into that person's psychological suffering, i.e., participating in their egoistic dramas. It should not, in other words, be equated with collapsing into and hence reproducing neurotic tendencies or emotional reactivity. Say, for instance, that your friend is in the hospital with a broken tibia (shinbone) and is feeling intensely grumpy and despondent. If at some point in the past you also have broken your leg, you'll now be able easily to empathize with *her* situation. And if not, you've almost certainly experienced a physical injury of some sort, so you know what she's going through. You can empathize and express concern. But this doesn't mean you also need to become grumpy and despondent.

True compassion is always, simultaneously, an expression of wisdom. It's the wisdom that knows, "This too shall pass." It's the wisdom that knows, "No matter what the injury or illness, in the core of your being, you're already and always perfect." It's the wisdom that's willing to listen deeply, all the way to the silence at the core of the anguished wailing. This wisdom is joyful, clear, and spacious. It's the healing balm your compassion skillfully offers (along with helping to change bandages and all sorts of other practical tasks). Don't leave home without it.

3. There's an upside to suffering.

When you notice that you're suffering, you're motivated to do something to change the situation. You feel the desire to move from suffering to happiness. This is great! In this sense, suffering serves a very noble purpose. Suffering says, "Hey! Can someone please help me wake up and smell the roses?" Sometimes this message is in code, but it's always there somewhere (engraved in tiny letters on the underside of the vase) if you look closely enough.

RAIN: Becoming Intimate with Pain

RAIN is a useful acronym to commit to memory as support for remembering how to relate skillfully to pain and suffering. It stands for:

Recognition

See the pain or suffering as pain or suffering. In other words, notice it, rather than trying to ignore or repress it.

Acceptance

Welcome the painful sensations or unpleasant emotions fully. Let them arise and dissolve as they do, without interference, within an attitude of benevolent indifference. Do your best to avoid engaging in push-pull dynamics: judging, rejecting, or clinging. Instead, just let them be clouds floating through the sky of your awareness.

Investigation

Let yourself be curious. Notice patterns within the painful sensations or unpleasant emotions. Become your own private investigator, passionate scientist, or endlessly curious child. Devise experiments. Learn things.

Nonidentification

Remember that the thoughts, emotions, and sensations are not who you essentially are. They're just aspects of a character (whom you refer to as "me") in the movie that's currently playing. And who are you if not this character? Perhaps the screen on which the movie is playing? Or the light of awareness flowing through the projector?

MEDITATION

Self-Compassion

In her book, *The Freedom of Being: At Ease With What Is*, Jan Frazier offers a beautiful piece of advice, rich with insight and compassion:

> We are free, and we don't know it. It feels the furthest thing from possible, that it could be so. We'd swear we're at the mercy of what goes wrong, what goes right.
>
> And yet (here is the truth), freedom is right here. So far away, it seems, but right here. Even as you could spend your whole life chasing it down, you have the scent of it on you all the while.
>
> The perfection is right alongside the mess, intimate with the misaligned mini-disaster that life appears to be. Close as the breath that's moving in you right now.

This meditation invites you to embrace, with tender friendliness and infinite compassion, "the perfection right alongside the mess" of your own body and mind, right here, right now. Nothing is excluded. All is welcome. This simple practice is one to come back to, again and again. It provides deep nourishment (which you deserve!) and is fertile ground for the flowering of insight into the impermanence of thoughts, emotions, and physical sensations.

Set your timer for five minutes, ten minutes, or longer. Press start. Place the timer next to you. Settle in, using the instructions on page 58.

1. **Find a comfortable reclining position.** Lie down on the floor, on your bed, or in a reclining easy chair.

2. **Hands on heart and belly.** Rest one hand gently on your heart-space and the other on your lower abdomen (below the navel). Let the quality of your touch be that of a mother soothing and comforting her child, or a trusted friend offering a tender hug.

3. **Abdominal breathing.** Feel your breath rising and falling into your abdomen. As you inhale, feel your belly pressing up gently into the palm of your hand. As you exhale, feel your belly relaxing back naturally toward your spine. Smile gently.

4. **Notice sensations, thoughts, and emotions.** Turn your attention inward, noticing physical sensations, thoughts, and emotions arising and dissolving. Let them do their dance without interference. Allow them to appear and disappear.

5. **Shower stuck places with compassion.** When you notice a physical sensation or emotional pattern that seems particularly sticky or constricted, use your breath to offer a rain of blessings. Inhale and notice the emotion or sensation. Exhale and direct a gentle stream of compassion—carried on the current of your breath—swirling into and around the emotion or sensation. Imagine it soaking, soothing, cleansing, nourishing, or doing whatever else is the perfect thing to do. Trust that the breath carries universal intelligence: It knows exactly what is needed.

6. **Understand that you're not alone.** Know that you're not the only one who feels this way. Countless other human beings also experience physical and emotional constrictions just like the one you're experiencing now. Feel your compassion expanding to include all others who are suffering in a similar way.

7. **Feel peace and space.** As you feel a physical constriction, be aware also of the space around and within it. As a physical constriction releases, feel it dissolving into the space around and within it. As you become aware of an unpleasant stuck emotion, be aware also of the peace around and within it. As a stuck emotion moves, feel it dissolving into the peace around and within it.

8. **Offer words of kindness and compassion.** Sing or whisper yourself a lullaby. Two to four short lines is perfect. For instance: "May I be safe. May I be peaceful. May I accept myself exactly as I am and revel in my inherent perfection." This is just an example. Let yours be the words you've always wanted to hear— what's most deliciously nourishing, sublimely supportive, perfect beyond perfect.

9. **Notice how you feel.** When your timer goes off, relax, take a couple of deep, slow breaths, and take note of any feelings or sensations that may have arisen. Notice also the spacious "sky" of awareness, within which these feelings or sensations arise and dissolve. Know that who you are, essentially, is this sky of awareness: infinitely expansive, unbounded, free.

Tips and Variations

- As you begin the practice, imagine yourself in what's sometimes referred to as a "power place": an environment that's especially nourishing and beautiful. This might be a place that you've actually been to (a mountain meadow or secluded cave), or it might be a place entirely imagined. Imagining yourself in this power place adds nourishment to the practice.

- This Self-Compassion meditation is designed to nourish comfort, ease, and relaxation. There may be moments, however, when you become aware of unpleasant sensations or difficult emotions. In the big picture, this is really good news! These are mental-emotional skeletons (associated with old storylines) coming out of their closets: unresolved wounds, in need of loving-kindness.

- While some of these stuck patterns may dissolve rather quickly, others will transform more slowly. This is natural, and there's no hurry. So don't hesitate—if you feel it's been enough for one day—to bring the meditation to a close. Take a walk outside, or listen to some beautiful music. Be kind to yourself after you sit with difficult thoughts and feelings.

66

Becoming intimate with pain is the key to changing at the core of our being—staying open to everything we experience, letting the sharpness of difficult times pierce us to the heart, letting these times open us, humble us, and make us wiser and more brave.

—Pema Chödrön, "Turn Your Thinking Upside Down"

─── TAKE TEN ───

Silencing Your Inner Critic

Whose voice is that? you wonder—the one that's always pointing out that what you just did is totally wrong or, at the very least, not quite right. The one that sometimes shouts, sometimes whines, sometimes whispers—but always with the same basic message: *You're just not quite up to par. You're flawed, and it's embarrassing. What's wrong with you?!*

Now is the perfect moment (*No, it isn't!* counters the inner critic) to practice the Self-Compassion meditation. Yes, it really is. So take a deep breath, and settle in. Rest one hand on your heart-space, the other on your belly. Say "ahh" to release the tension in your jaw. Breathe.

Allow the voice of the inner critic to arise. Allow the emotions that it triggers to arise. Can you experience the emotions as simply bursts of life-force energy? Can you hear the inner critic's words as simply sound—a kind of music, like a Mozart string quartet, just not quite as harmonious? If so, great. If not, no problem. Simply notice and allow the thoughts and emotions to be, like the sky allowing clouds space to float.

And now offer words of kindness and compassion to yourself. The inner critic is just one member of the committee. Now it's time to give the floor to your inner advocate: the one who offers words of support. You write the script, and you step into that role. Even better, let it be Wisdom Mind that's speaking. You know how to do it. Say, "I love you unconditionally." Say, "You are primordially pure." Say, "No human being is perfect, and I love and accept you just the way you are."

MEDITATION

Tonglen (Giving and Taking)

Once you feel comfortable "RAINing" compassion upon your-self—recognizing, accepting, investigating, and not interfering with your thoughts and emotions—you may feel ready for the challenge of Tonglen, a type of meditation practiced in Tibetan Buddhism. Tonglen practice is sometimes referred to as "giving and taking." What's revolutionary about Tonglen is its bold invitation for you to reverse your habitual tendency to push away pain and suffering and conversely to hold on to comfort, ease, and pleasure in a stingy way.

Instead of hoarding what's good, you'll be invited to give it away freely. Instead of looking away or putting up a protective bar-rier against someone else's pain and suffering, you'll be invited to embrace it fully.

In Tonglen practice, you learn how to willingly (and with great joy!) take in the pain and suffering of another; and then—in the spirit of offering a gift—send out spaciousness and relief. Tonglen is powerful medicine. It's the needle that can pop the bubble of self-centeredness, revealing a previously hidden sky, blue and unbounded.

And now, without further ado, set your timer for five minutes, ten minutes, or longer. Press start. Place the timer next to you. Settle in, using the instructions on page 58.

1. **Rest in open brightness.** Rest quietly for a minute or two, tuning in to a sense of openness and stillness deep within and all around you: silent, bright, spacious.

2. **Practice how it feels to take and give.** As you inhale, imag-ine drawing in feelings that are dark, hot, sticky, and heavy. As you exhale, imagine extending a sense of refreshment—feelings that are bright, cool, light as a feather. Inhale the

Blowing Bubbles

*Each drama created by the monkey mind is like a bubble you
live in for a little while (an hour, a day, a decade, a lifetime). It's
a whole little world spun out of your mind in the manner a spider
spins a web or a child blows a bubble.*

*Creating bubble worlds is not necessarily a problem, as long as
you remain aware that this is what you're doing. Then it's just
a fun expression of creative energy. The problem arises when
you think that your bubble world is actually the entire universe,
the whole unbounded cosmos. And this, of course, is simply a
delusion. To live in a bubble without knowing it's a bubble is a
bummer. It's cramped and claustrophobic, though you somehow
don't quite notice this.*

*All the practices in this book can support you in seeing through—
and perhaps even popping—the bubble of self-centeredness.
Tonglen tends to be especially effective in this regard because
it directly challenges the assumption of a rigid distinction
between "self" and "other." It's this self/other separation that,
when taken to be ultimately and rigidly true, is the linchpin of
egoistic self-centeredness and the suffering it creates.*

yucky feelings and sensations through every pore of your
skin. Exhale in the manner of radiating brightness—shining
out light from every cell of your body, like an expanding
ripple from the center of a clear, quiet pond. Continue
synchronizing the taking and giving with the rhythm of
your breathing.

3. **Apply to a specific situation.** Apply the practice to a particular situation in your life. It's best to begin with someone you love and care for and naturally wish to help. Bring to mind the pain and suffering this person is experiencing. Now, as you inhale, imagine drawing that pain and suffering out of them, relieving them of this burden. As you exhale, imagine offering comfort and ease, along with whatever specific remedies would be helpful.

4. **Expand to include others.** Extend the range of the giving and taking by including others who are in the same boat. If you're doing the practice for your aunt who has cancer, imagine including all other people who, like your aunt, are suffering with cancer. Breathe in their pain. Exhale a sense of comfort and ease.

5. **Notice how you feel.** When your timer goes off, relax, take a couple of deep, slow breaths, and take note of any feelings or sensations that may have arisen.

How did that go? Tonglen can be a bit challenging at first, though over time, it becomes quite pleasurable. Your compassion naturally expands, as does the insight that things are not as solid and fixed as you may have assumed. You find yourself more and more able to be there for others, to offer a helping hand, in a variety of situations.

Variation

■   In step 3, if you're feeling stuck, you can use an instance of your own pain and suffering as an anchor. For instance: Breathe in the feelings of inadequacy that you've been experiencing, while at the same time imagining that you're taking in the feelings of inadequacy of other people who are struggling in a similar way. Then with the exhalation, breathe out a sense of ease and confidence to yourself as well as to these other people.

Further Exploration

- Tonglen practice can be as simple as seeing the suffering of a homeless person begging on the street—or a young child being coarsely berated by their raging parent—and then with a deep inhalation taking in that pain—and with the next exhalation sending spacious comfort and relief. A single breath, dropping you into compassion and clarity.

- Don't worry, you aren't *really* going to take on another person's illness or injury. While there may be the rare, occasional saint who is actually able to absorb into their own physical body the illness or injury of another, these sorts of capacities arise only in those who have fully dissolved the perception of a difference between "self" and "other." In such cases, it's as though the left hand burns itself, and the right hand immediately offers comfort and relief. The right hand has no thought of being contaminated by the injury or illness of the left hand, nor does it feel arrogant in relation to its ability to help. It just naturally renders aid, in whatever way it can.

- Tonglen is a practice for transforming your mind—for replacing old dualistic patterns of grasping and repulsion with new "giving and taking" patterns that are more closely aligned with reality. While it can be profoundly healing for the one who's doing it—and its benefits tend to mysteriously ripple out in all directions—it's not a replacement for medical care.

> 66
>
> *Surrender something out of love and you'll get ten thousand times what you have surrendered. Surrender everything out of love and you get the infinite in return.*
>
> —Francis Lucille, unpublished transcript (www.francislucille.com)

TAKE TEN

Witnessing the Suffering
of a Loved One

Your twelve-year-old son has just broken his ankle. It happened during a soccer game—an innocent collision with an opposing team member, coupled with a rough spot on the field—and next thing you knew, there you were with him in the back of the ambulance. Now, after a simple surgery in which the bones were set, his leg is in a cast and propped up on pillows in the hospital bed.

The doctors have assured you that a full recovery is expected; the bones may even be stronger than before. Nevertheless, your heart goes out to him. He's in considerable physical pain and convinced that his dream of becoming the next Cristiano Renaldo or Lionel Messi is now forever lost. You want to help, but don't know how.

Now is the perfect moment to practice Tonglen. Take a couple of deep, slow breaths. Tune in to a sense of spacious quiet, deep within. Just for a moment, let go of thinking.

And now, begin the practice of taking and giving: As you inhale, imagine taking in your son's physical pain and emotional suffering. As you exhale, imagine sending physical comfort and mental ease to him. As you inhale, absorb his feelings of discouragement. As you exhale, send a wave of hope. As you inhale, take in his anger and confusion. As you exhale, send peace. Continue in this vein for five or ten minutes—and then notice how you feel.

MEDITATION

Flowing into the Gap

Imagine standing on earth, seeing a sky filled with clouds. It's Shropshire, England—which means that clouds are the sky's default setting. You've lived here all your life. Then one day, something miraculous happens. You see a patch of blue emerging from the silver-gray. Initially you think, *What a beautiful blue cloud that is!* You can't imagine it being anything else. Then another blue cloud appears, and then another. And they merge together.

All of a sudden, it dawns on you that what you're seeing is not a blue cloud, but rather sky. For the first time, you're seeing the sky in its natural state. For the first time, you recognize that the clouds you've been seeing all of your life have a background of sky.

This story illustrates the dawning of mindfulness: the transition from identifying with thoughts to simply observing them floating through the sky of your awareness. There are three stages to this process: (1) standing on earth, looking up, and assuming that the sky is nothing but clouds (that is, believing that the patterns of thought and emotion define who you are essentially); (2) realizing that sky is the background of clouds—that clouds arise and dissolve within the sky (that is, tuning in to the awareness aspect of your being, which is the dawning of mindfulness); and (3) shifting your point of view from that of someone standing on the earth and looking skyward to that of actually *being the sky* through which the clouds are floating (and then noticing that the actual substance of the clouds is nothing but sky). Another way of describing this third phase is that you come to understand that monkey mind is simply an aspect of the energy of Wisdom Mind. In other words, the monkeys, *in their essence*, are none other than Wisdom Mind: they are no less divine than any other "thing" in the *You-niverse*!

Toggling back and forth between these two points of view (looking at the sky and being the sky) is kind of like the well-known optical illusion of seeing two faces looking at each other in profile, and then seeing a vase outlined in the space between them. Both are there in the picture. Which one you see just depends on the angle of your glance or who knows what else. It kind of just happens, though there are ways of gently inviting the transition.

In this practice, you'll play with making this transition. Set your timer for five minutes, ten minutes, or longer. Press start. Place the timer next to you. Settle in, using the instructions on page 58.

1. **Notice a thought or image.** Become aware of a thought or an internal image appearing like a cloud within the sky of your awareness.

2. **Notice the thought or image dissolving.** At some point, the thought or image will dissolve. Notice this happening.

3. **Hang out in the gap.** As the thought or image dissolves—like a cloud dissolving into the sky—dissolve with it, and then simply hang out in the space that remains. At some point, another thought or image will arise, at which point you can repeat the process: noticing the thought, noticing it dissolving, and then hanging out in the gap between the thoughts.

4. **Notice how you feel.** When your timer goes off, relax, take a couple of deep, slow breaths, and take note of any feelings or sensations that may have arisen.

Further Exploration

■   Though this practice is simple, it's not necessarily easy. So be patient, gentle, and kind with yourself. There's no hurry. It's here for you to play with whenever you feel inspired.

■   As you cultivate the capacity to flow into the gap, your compassion will naturally deepen and expand. You'll notice that it has two distinct flavors: (1) compassion in relation to the particular physical, mental, and emotional difficulties that folks are experiencing—you wish they could be free from these unpleasant circumstances—and (2) Compassion in relation to the belief that such difficulties define who the person is, essentially. You wish for them the spacious understanding that knows the circumstances are fleeting and ephemeral, like clouds passing through the sky.

> 66
>
> *Life is this simple: we are living in a world that is absolutely transparent and the divine is shining through it all the time. This is not just a nice story or a fable; it is true.*
>
> —Thomas Merton, *Essential Writings*

Your compassion may take the shape of aspirations such as "May your thundering storm clouds be transformed into softly billowing and infinitely friendly cumulous clouds," or "May your cloudy sky reveal patches of blue," or "May you come to know yourself as the sky."

─────────── TAKE TEN ───────────

Driving in Heavy Traffic

It's rush hour. It's 97 degrees outside. The air conditioning in your car stopped working yesterday. Coming around the highway's bend, you see a veritable sea of red taillights ahead. You brake, slow to a snaking five miles per hour, and then come to a stop. It's bumper to bumper as far as you can see. The muscles around your jaw are quivering. Your temples throb beneath beads of sweat.

Now is the perfect moment to flow into the gap. (After all, where else is there to go?) Take a deep, slow inhalation. Exhale completely, saying "ahh" to release the tension in your jaw. Smile gently. Turn your attention inward. Notice the arising of thoughts and emotions. Notice where they're flowing smoothly—sailing along your mind's highway at a cool 75 miles per hour. And then notice where they've clumped, become a bit jammed, and stuck—glued together by sticky emotions and seething toxic fumes.

Now tune your attention to noticing a single thought or image. See it arise. And then see it dissolve. And as this thought or image dissolves, dissolve with it—and then just hang out in that space, that openness. Continue this practice for as long as it takes for the traffic to start moving again. If so inspired (from the spaciousness of the gap), send out thoughts of loving-kindness to the drivers of the cars around you.

And remember: While the gap between your car and the next may all but vanish, the gap between your thoughts is always deep and vast. It is an infinite expanse, there for you to flow into, whenever the spirit moves you.

MEDITATION

Forgiveness

Like the Appreciation and Gratitude meditation you practiced earlier, this forgiveness meditation is rooted in the insight that separation isn't real. We're not isolated entities, completely cut off from others, but rather are interconnected in countless ways. We share a single world, a single atmosphere, a single heart of reality. We're never really separate, which is why holding a grudge, harboring resentment, seeking revenge, or being scornfully excluded feels so uncomfortable. Such actions and attitudes are out of alignment with reality.

> 66
>
> *Its door opens near. It's a shrine*
> *by the road, it's a flower in the parking lot*
> *of The Pentagon, it says, "Look around,*
> *listen. Feel the air."*
>
> —William Stafford, "Poetry"

Meditations to generate appreciation, gratitude, compassion, and forgiveness are powerful because they're in alignment with reality—the reality of our interbeing. As this insight of interbeing ripens, it becomes natural to let go of heavy-handed judgments. As judgment is released, appreciation, gratitude, and forgiveness flow naturally. More and more, you become able to forgive—to "give back" to the infinite intelligence of the universe, the thing, or person you've been holding in judgment.

When your right hand wields a hammer and accidentally whacks the thumb of your left hand, does your left thumb file a formal grievance and then hold a grudge for two decades against your right hand? Of course not! Remember:

- Holding a grudge is like drinking poison and believing that it's going to kill your enemy.

- Hurling an invective is like throwing a steaming ball of crap at the person you hate. Depending on your aim, and on how skillful that person is at dodging bullets (or becoming the space through which they travel), it may or may not soil your enemy. But with 100 percent certainty it's going to make a smelly mess out of your hand.

Forgiveness is a good thing. This meditation will support you in forgiving those you may still find it challenging to forgive.

Set your timer for five minutes, ten minutes, or longer. Press start. Place the timer next to you. Settle in, using the instructions on page 58.

✱
Dodging bullets is easier than you think. *Remember Neo in* The Matrix *dodging bullets, and then at the very end just stopping them in midair? This provides a great visual metaphor for how you can dodge the "bullets" of insults, judgments, and other emotional daggers. Much better than donning a bulletproof vest (clamping on your emotional armor) is to become the sky—the neutral witness of thoughts and emotions—through which those bullets pass. When they find no place to land, no place to lodge, they have no way of creating a wound. When there's no wound, there's nothing that needs to be forgiven.*

1. **Bring to mind a person with whom you have some "unfinished business."** This might be someone you've been holding a grudge against and would like to forgive. Conversely, it may be someone you feel you owe an apology. Best to start with relatively minor grievances, and work your way up to the more difficult ones, as you become more adept.

2. **Imagine this person as a tiny "light-being," floating in your *hara* (lower abdomen) or in your heart-space.** Create an image of this person—like a tiny fairy or cartoon figure—no more than one-half inch high and made entirely of light. Invite this tiny image into your heart-space, or the space of your *hara*, as if you were inviting someone into your sunroom for tea. Choose whichever location feels most comfortable to you. Imagine this tiny light-being floating within the vast space of your heart-space or *hara* and being nourished by that light.

3. **Forgive or ask for forgiveness.** Now say, "I'm sorry, please forgive me. Please welcome me back into your heart." Or say, "I forgive you. I forgive you completely. I forgive you unconditionally. I welcome you back into my heart." Repeat these words internally, imagining them being directed to the light-being floating in your heart-space or *hara*. See the little light-being receiving the words and accepting them.

4. **Dissolve the light-being back into light.** When the practice feels complete, thank the light-being for its visit. Then imagine it floating out of your heart-space or *hara* and dissolving into the light of the surrounding environment.

5. **Notice how you feel.** When your timer goes off, relax, take a couple of deep, slow breaths, and take note of any feelings or sensations that may have arisen.

Variation

■ For self-forgiveness, repeat this meditation with all its steps, but imagine a tiny version of yourself, rather than of another person. Forgive yourself or ask yourself for forgiveness. Then, to bring the practice to a close, allow that tiny light-being version of yourself to dissolve, to merge completely into the energy of your *hara* or heart-space.

> 66
>
> *The emergence and blossoming of understanding, love and intelligence has nothing to do with any tradition, no matter how ancient or impressive—it has nothing to do with time. It happens completely on its own when a human being questions, wonders, listens and looks without getting stuck in fear, pleasure and pain. When self-concern is quiet, in abeyance, heaven and earth are open. The mystery, the essence of all life is not separate from the silent openness of simple listening.*
>
> —Toni Packer, *The Light of Discovery*

TAKE TEN

Forgiving Someone Who Hurt You

The phone rings. You can tell by the way the person asks for you—in that curtly mechanical yet insistent voice—that it's someone representing a large corporation. You were right. It's the company that financed the loan you agreed to cosign with your sister years ago. They're telling you that your sister has not been making the payments, and that you—as her *cosigner*—are now responsible for the debt.

After hanging up the phone, utterly stunned by this news, you feel a wave of panicked nausea. You feel betrayed. Outraged and hurt deeply. How could she do such a thing? She promised to take full responsibility for repaying this loan. You knew she had some flakey tendencies, but never did you imagine it would come to this. It feels absolutely unforgivable. You think, *That's it, we're finished.* You feel a seething rage sinking deep into your bones, and so much sadness.

This is a perfect moment to work with the Forgiveness meditation. Sit down. Take several long, deep breaths, and say "ahh" to release the tension in your jaw. Imagine your sister as a tiny light-being. Follow the steps in the meditation. When time is up, notice how you feel, now that the toxic poison of hatred, rage, and resentment has (at least in part) drained away. Receive deeply the healing balm of love and forgiveness, as it's working in your body right now.

Repeat this practice once a day for a week. Then, from your new clarity and openhearted emotional neutrality, decide how to proceed.

MEDITATION

Getting Naked

You may recall the advice on perceiving nakedly from the "How to Plant Seeds of Mindfulness" discussion on page 44. Coming full circle, we're now going to explore more deeply what it means to perceive nakedly, and how to go about actually doing it. The Italian sculptor Michelangelo once said: "In every block of marble I see a statue as plain as though it stood before me, shaped and perfect in attitude and action. I have only to hew away the rough walls that imprison the lovely apparition to reveal it to the other eyes as mine see it."

Michelangelo is describing the process of creating a sculpture as one of simply freeing the statue that already exists within the block of marble. So you could think of Michelangelo's *David* as already being there in the block of marble. Michelangelo's job was not so much to construct as it was to free *David*—to liberate him from the block of marble in which he was trapped.

Perceiving nakedly is something similar to liberating *David*. It's chipping away at all the beliefs and concepts that prevent you from seeing directly—nakedly—the beauty that is already here and being fully intimate with it. It's removing what is extraneous, just like Michelangelo did, to unveil *David*.

So, don't be a blockhead! The larger piece of "creating" a beautiful world is simply not covering it up with unnecessary judgments and evaluations. Rather, just let it be. Let it reveal its inherent beauty, and honor and appreciate what's already here.

What we love about the innocence of a young child is the freshness and spontaneity that comes with perceiving nakedly. They're naturally enamored with the magic of the universe, and it's infectious! What's great is that you can recover this ability, no matter your age.

> " *But when you move amidst the world of sense, free from*
> *attachment and aversion alike, there comes the peace in*
> *which all sorrows end, and you live in the wisdom of the Self.*
>
> —Bhagavad Gita 2:64

You'll be applying five simple labels, corresponding to the five main sensory channels, as follows:

Touch

To each tactile sensation, you'll apply the label "touch." So, for instance, if you notice the feeling your foot contacting the floor, you'll say, "Touch."

Sight

To each visual sensation, you'll apply the label "sight." So, for instance, if you notice a leaf gently quivering on its branch or a shadow on the wall, you'll say, "Sight."

Sound

To each auditory sensation, you'll apply the label "sound." If you notice the chirping of a bird or the sound of your breath, you'll say, "Sound."

Taste

To each gustatory sensation, you'll apply the label "taste." If you notice the taste of peppermint from brushing your teeth, you'll say, "Taste."

Smell

To each olfactory sensation, you'll apply the label "smell." If you notice the scent of an almond croissant being warmed in the oven or the aftershave of the man sitting in front of you, you'll say, "Smell."

So now, without further ado, set your timer for five minutes, ten minutes, or longer. Press start. Place the timer next to you. Settle in, using the instructions on page 58.

1. **Note and label sights, sounds, tactile sensations, tastes, and smells.** Get into a rhythm of applying one of these five labels every five seconds or so. The idea is to stay at this level of bare attention—of perceiving nakedly. This means just being aware of the act of perceiving itself prior to naming the perception as this thing or that, and then constructing a story out of those named things. The mind has a strong habit of racing from the immediate perception (say, the "sight" of a green leaf) into assigning a name ("green leaf"), and then telling a story ("the leaf is green because it's summer, but I really prefer the colors of autumn"). For now, see if you can resist this temptation to "clothe" your experience in names and conceptual elaboration. Instead, stay with just perceiving nakedly.

2. **Explore specific sensory channels.** If you'd like, you can narrow your noting to just one or two sensory channels. So, for instance, you could decide to just notice and label "sight" and "sound." This doesn't mean that the other sensory channels won't be active; of course they will. It just means that you're tuning in to sight and sound, via the labeling process, and letting the others be in the background.

3.   **Notice how you feel.** When your timer goes off, relax, enjoy a couple of deep breaths, and notice any feelings or sensations that are arising. Notice also the aware presence that remains as sensations come and go.

Variation

- "Go naked" to a concert or museum. Devote 10 minutes or longer to the Getting Naked meditation. Then, infused with the fragrance of these explorations, listen to some beautiful music or gaze at beautiful paintings or sculpture (such as Michelangelo's *David*). Every now and again, as you're sitting in the concert hall or strolling through the museum, drop back into the formal Getting Naked meditation practice for just a minute or two (no one has to know you're doing it), then return again to simply enjoying the music, enjoying *David*.

Tip

- Experiment with perceiving nakedly during walking meditation: a wonderful combination! You can also try it for five minutes at the start of a meal or for ten minutes before making love.

─── TAKE TEN ───

Staying Focused Under Pressure

You may not be Serena Williams, and this may not be Wimbledon, but still, within your world, it's important. It's the adult division of the Nebraska State tennis championships, and you've made it to the final for the first time. The match is scheduled to begin in just under two hours.

You can't remember ever being quite this nervous. Not just one or two, but an entire kaleidoscope of butterflies is fluttering in your stomach. Images of last year's semifinal defeat flash their neon warnings. Suddenly you feel downright nauseated, a clench of panic, cotton in your mouth.

This is a perfect moment to play with perceiving nakedly. Sit or lie down. Take several long, deep breaths, saying "ahh" with the exhalations, to release tension in your face, neck, and jaw.

And now, begin to notice sights, sounds, and tactile sensations as they arise within and around you. To each moment of noticing, apply a label: "sight" or "sound" or "touch." If your mind wanders, no problem; remember, that's the "magic moment." Just come back to sight, sound, and touch, again and again. Continue for 10 or 15 minutes. Notice how you feel.

Yes, a tennis match requires a certain amount of thinking. But mostly it's just the skillful flowing through sight, sound, and touch, trusting that your cultivated capacities will come to the fore exactly when they're needed. Good luck!

Flow with whatever is happening and let your mind be free.
Stay centered by accepting whatever you are doing.
This is the ultimate.

—Zhuangzi, *The Collected Writings*

CHAPTER EIGHT

Nurturing Your Meditation Practice

Well, congratulations! You've made it through seven of eight chapters. That's awesome. And now, as a final send-off, this chapter will be a care package of sorts: some friendly advice for creating a daily practice, for setting up a mini-retreat, and for keeping things fresh and flowing, as you allow your meditation practice, little by little, to infuse every aspect of your life.

A daily meditation practice is like a goose that lays golden eggs. It may seem—for days or weeks on end—like nothing much is happening. But then, voilà! You experience a golden egg of insight, a new way of seeing things, a moment of true intimacy.

So, take good care of this goose. But don't hold it so tightly that you strangle it. In other words, make a firm commitment (build a nest), but also keep your daily practice well fed with the nourishing energies of ease and curiosity, spontaneous explorations, and the like.

Tips and Suggestions for Establishing a Daily Practice

We've touched on these suggestions earlier, but let's summarize them again here:

Same Time, Same Place. What works best for most beginners is to make meditation part of their daily routine: the same time, same place, from three to six days out of seven.

A Nourishing, Beautiful, Sacred Space. A pleasant and uplifting atmosphere for your meditation practice can be a huge support. When you enter such an environment, your body and mind say, "Ahh—yes, thank you!"

Three to Six Days Out of Seven: Firm Yet Flexible. Take your lead from the goose that lays golden eggs: The best kind of nest is one that is firm (a circular weave of sticks and downy feathers) yet also flexible (soft enough to be comfy and to survive a strong windstorm). Leave one day of the week for being totally spontaneous: lazy, wild, wandering, or whatever.

Notice How You Feel Before and After Your Meditation Session. This important information will motivate you to continue or change course as needed.

Support from Friends and Teachers. Having a practice buddy—or two or three—can be a great support. Each of you practices in your own space, but you touch base every now and then just to see how the other is doing. If you feel stuck, ready for added inspiration, or hungry for a deeper challenge, seek the company of a teacher or someone who's farther along the path than you are. This is like being a traveler on a trip to Paris and seeking advice from someone who has lived in France their entire life. As a native to the city, this person can offer directions to little-known but truly excellent restaurants, let you know which neighborhoods to avoid, and provide answers to questions you didn't even know you had. This person can be a treasure chest of tips and shortcuts, which add immeasurably to the efficiency and pleasure of your journey.

Knowing Which Meditation Technique to Use

So many choices: In this book alone, there are over 30 meditations. And beyond the boundaries of this book, there are hundreds if not thousands more. And with such bounty, the most skillful way to proceed is to choose just a few practices: those that, to your eye, appear to be the most nourishing and delicious. Put these on your plate. Then sit down, relax, and enjoy your meal.

As you revisit the practices in this book, here's a simple three-step process that will serve you well:

1. **Follow your bliss.** Pick the one practice you most enjoy, feel intuitively drawn to, and find yourself enthused about exploring more deeply.

2. **Make a provisional commitment.** Decide to practice this technique for a given amount of time—anywhere between two weeks and two months is a good rule of thumb—and then stick with it through thick and thin. Creating this temporal container is like a scientist setting up their laboratory within which they conduct the experiment. Without the laboratory, the experiment can't happen. And it would be a bit strange to set up the laboratory and then decide to not conduct the experiment. So stay with the program for at least two weeks. Give the goose a chance to do what she does.

3. **Reevaluate.** After consistently practicing for the length of time you've chosen, pause to take stock: How are you feeling? Does the practice still hold your attention? Is it unfolding in a way that feels beneficial? If all is well, keep going. If need be, change course by going back to the first of these three steps.

The Dynamic Duos

If you prefer toggling back and forth between two practices, here are some pairings that are naturally resonant. Feel free, of course, to create your own alliances.

Focus on Breath & Letting Go of Thoughts—pages 14 and 60

Appreciation and Gratitude & Forgiveness—pages 103 and 136

Inner Smile & Appreciation and Gratitude—pages 95 and 103

Walking with Mindfulness & Getting Naked—pages 77 and 141

Letting Go of Thoughts & Flowing into the Gap—pages 60 and 132

Scanning the Body & Inner Smile—pages 68 and 95

Self-Compassion & Focus on Rest—pages 122 and 114

Loving-Kindness & Tonglen—pages 99 and 127

> 66
>
> *Life and death are of supreme importance.*
>
> *Time swiftly passes by and opportunity is lost.*
>
> *Each of us should strive to awaken. Awaken.*
>
> *Take heed, do not squander your life.*
>
> —Dogen, *Shobogenzo*

28-Day Meditation Plans

Sometimes, a clearly structured plan is what feels most useful. If this is true for you, then consider using one of these. As you'll see, each plan includes a nice amount of variety, while emphasizing the cultivation of specific qualities.

Plan Rules

- Commit to ten minutes of meditation per day, six days out of seven, with one "lazy day." (The "lazy day" doesn't have to be Saturday—but keep it consistent from week to week.)

- The first week will be devoted to the Focus on Breath and Letting Go of Thoughts meditations. This will help establish a stable foundation for your practice.

- Weeks two, three, and four will include exercises geared specifically to the particular theme of the plan.

- At the beginning of the week, read through the instructions for the meditations that you'll be exploring. This way, you'll need just a quick reminder as you sit down to practice.

- Make a photocopy of the plan's chart—or copy and paste into an electronic file—and check off each day as you complete the practice.

28 Days of Deep Nourishment

This is the perfect plan for times of duress, such as when you're going through a painful breakup, or caring for someone who is gravely ill.

WEEK 1

Sunday: Focus on Breath (page 14)

Monday: Letting Go of Thoughts (page 60)

Tuesday: Focus on Breath

Wednesday: Letting Go of Thoughts

Thursday: Focus on Breath

Friday: Walking with Mindfulness (page 77)

Saturday: Lazy Day

WEEK 2

Sunday: Focus on Breath

Monday: Scanning the Body (page 68)

Tuesday: Inner Smile (page 95)

Wednesday: Scanning the Body

Thursday: Inner Smile

Friday: Walking with Mindfulness

Saturday: Lazy Day

WEEK 3

Sunday: Focus on Breath

Monday: Self-Compassion (page 122)

Tuesday: Focus on Rest (page 114)

Wednesday: Self-Compassion

Thursday: Focus on Rest

Friday: Walking with Mindfulness

Saturday: Lazy Day

WEEK 4

Sunday: Focus on Breath

Monday: Self-Compassion

Tuesday: Forgiveness (page 136)

Wednesday: Self-Compassion

Thursday: Forgiveness

Friday: Walking with Mindfulness

Saturday: Lazy Day

28 Days of Happiness

A great plan for when you've got a case of the winter blues, are stuck in a rut at work, or are just feeling a general sense of boredom or malaise.

WEEK 1

Sunday: Focus on Breath (page 14)

Monday: Letting Go of Thoughts (page 60)

Tuesday: Focus on Breath

Wednesday: Letting Go of Thoughts

Thursday: Focus on Breath

Friday: Walking with Mindfulness (page 77)

Saturday: Lazy Day

WEEK 2

Sunday: Focus on Breath

Monday: Scanning the Body (page 68)

Tuesday: Inner Smile (page 95)

Wednesday: Scanning the Body

Thursday: Inner Smile

Friday: Walking with Mindfulness

Saturday: Lazy Day

WEEK 3

Sunday: Focus on Breath

Monday: Loving-Kindness (page 99)

Tuesday: Sympathetic Joy (page 109)

Wednesday: Loving-Kindness

Thursday: Sympathetic Joy

Friday: Walking with Mindfulness

Saturday: Lazy Day

WEEK 4

Sunday: Focus on Breath

Monday: Focus on Rest (page 114)

Tuesday: Getting Naked (page 141)

Wednesday: Focus on Rest

Thursday: Getting Naked

Friday: Walking with Mindfulness

Saturday: Lazy Day

28 Days of Relaxation

A great plan for when your work schedule feels overwhelming and your to-do list seems endless.

WEEK 1

Sunday: Focus on Breath (page 14)

Monday: Letting Go of Thoughts (page 60)

Tuesday: Focus on Breath

Wednesday: Letting Go of Thoughts

Thursday: Focus on Breath

Friday: Walking with Mindfulness (page 77)

Saturday: Lazy Day

WEEK 2

Sunday: Focus on Breath

Monday: Focus on a Candle Flame (page 72)

Tuesday: Inner Smile (page 95)

Wednesday: Focus on a Candle Flame

Thursday: Inner Smile

*Friday:*Walking with Mindfulness

Saturday: Lazy Day

WEEK 3

Sunday: Focus on Breath

Monday: Self-Compassion (page 122)

Tuesday: Focus on Rest (page 114)

Wednesday: Self-Compassion

Thursday: Focus on Rest

Friday: Walking with Mindfulness

Saturday: Lazy Day

WEEK 4

Sunday: Focus on Breath

Monday: Letting Go of Thoughts

Tuesday: Flowing into the Gap (page 132)

Wednesday: Focus on Rest

Thursday: Focus on Rest

Friday: Walking with Mindfulness

Saturday: Lazy Day

Your Mini-Meditation Retreat

It can be a sweet adventure, and deeply beneficial, to go away for a weekend or longer to attend a formal meditation retreat. You can also create a retreat in your own home. Occasional in-home retreats are an excellent way of deepening your practice. The logistics are relatively simple—no traveling or extra expenses. All that's required is the willingness to devote a half day or full day to your meditation explorations. Here's how:

- Choose a day, and mark your calendar.
- Invite a practice buddy, or decide to do it solo.
- Create a schedule and then dive in.

Here's a sample schedule for a half-day retreat, beginning at 9 a.m. and ending at 1 p.m.

9:00 to 9:20	Focus on Breath meditation
9:20 to 9:30	Walking with Mindfulness
9:30 to 9:50	Letting Go of Thoughts meditation
9:50 to 10:00	Walking with Mindfulness
10:00 to 10:20	Focus on Breath meditation
10:20 to 10:30	Walking with Mindfulness
10:30 to 10:50	Letting Go of Thoughts meditation
10:50 to 11:00	Walking with Mindfulness
11:00 to 11:15	Tea break
11:15 to 11:30	Walking with Mindfulness
11:30 to 11:50	Letting Go of Thoughts meditation
11:50 to 12:00	Walking with Mindfulness
12:00 to 12:40	Focus on Breath meditation
12:40 to 1:00	Walking with Mindfulness

Final Words of Encouragement

Here are some nuggets of inspiration and gentle-fierce encouragement from two illustrious meditators from the past who you can now rightly consider your ancestors: Dogen and Milarepa.

Milarepa was a Tibetan yogi, poet, and meditation master known for his beautiful voice and modest wardrobe (just a simple white cotton cloth). During one part of his life, when he was doing a lot of meditating up in a mountain cave, he ate mostly nettles, and his skin took on a rather greenish hue. He offers the following advice: "The affairs of the world will go on forever. Do not delay the practice of meditation. Once you have met with the profound instructions from a meditation master, with single pointed determination, set about realizing the Truth."

Dogen was a Japanese Zen meditation master. His parents died when he was very young—a poignant reminder of the impermanence of all things. Dogen's deepest interest was in reconciling the fact of our inherent perfection with the need for meditation practice: If we're already perfect, why do we need to practice? He said: "Life and death are of supreme importance. Time swiftly passes by and opportunity is lost. Each of us should strive to awaken. Awaken. Take heed, do not squander your life."

It's nice to be inspired by illustrious practitioners such as these. It's also good to keep in mind that your journey is your very own. Value each step, and delight in the tiniest of openings, the smallest of insights. Think of these as delicate rays of light, illuminating the stained-glass windows of your mind.

Following is a short, and by no means comprehensive, list of things to celebrate when you make a meditation practice a regular part of your life. If any or all of these have started emerging since you began this book, in large or small ways, that's great! If not, have patience and trust that—like flower bulbs during winter—the time is just not quite ripe, but spring is on its way.

- Increased feelings of peace and joy, or a subtle current of contentment flowing just beneath the surface of your various activities.
- Nonreactivity: Things that used to push your buttons don't any longer, or at least not as much or as often.
- More spontaneity and playfulness.
- Moments of feeling intimate with experiences. In other words, increased sensitivity to sights, sounds, tastes, smells, and touches.

- A piquing of curiosity—and a sense of wonder and awe—in relation to things large (the Milky Way) and small (a ladybug, so red against the lawn's ocean of green).

- A sense of impending delight replaces the sense of impending doom, more and more: I wonder what excellent thing is going to happen next?

Producing Your Own Movie

Through the practices in this book, you're learning how to watch the movie of monkey mind—or just ordinary life—unfolding as it does without the interference of judgments and unquestioned beliefs. To some degree, at least, you can also play with making your own movies and with cultivating attitudes that nourish and empower. Here are some possible roles for you to play and humble suggestions for scripts to use just to prime the pump of your imagination. (Take them or leave them, as you wish.) As you continue your meditation journey:

- Be a scientist, using the telescope of pure awareness, the microscope of mindfulness.

- Be a deep-sea diver, enjoying the stillness of the depths, the choppy waves on the surface, and everything in between.

- Be a lepidopterist, one who studies butterflies, examining all your delicate, fleeting thoughts and feelings.

- Be a spelunker, lighting up the subterranean crevices of your mind. *Oh, look, a crystalline stalagmite!*

- Be a pastry chef extraordinaire, creating recipes for almond croissants and lasting happiness alike. *Yum!*

- Be bold. What do you have to lose?

- Be infinitely patient and kind with yourself and others.

- Be yourself—as if it could be otherwise.

APPENDIX: SUN SALUTATION YOGA SEQUENCE

1. In Mountain Pose, smile gently, reach down through the soles of your feet, and tune in to a sense of brightness in the heart-space. Enjoy several rounds of breathing.

2. As you extend your arms upward with the inhalation, imagine connecting the brightness of your heart-space with that of the sun, in a gesture of celebration and gratitude.

3. As you exhale, fold forward, aware now of the brightness in your hips as they open.

4. Inhaling, step right foot back to a lunge.

5. Exhaling, bring left foot back to plank position—and with the next inhalation, feel your spine lengthening.

6. With the exhale, drop knees and then chest to the floor, keeping hips gently lifted, and feeling brightness in the heart-space.

7. As you inhale, reach chin and chest forward into Cobra Pose, with front of pelvis anchored on the floor.

8. Exhale into Downward Dog, aware of the brightness in your hips and belly, as sitting-bones lift skyward, and heels reach back and down.

9. Inhaling, step right foot forward to a lunge.

10. Exhaling, step left foot forward (next to right foot) and fold forward, feeling the brightness in your hips.

11. Inhaling, reach arms out and up, offering the brightness in your heart-space to the sun, in a gesture of joyful appreciation.

12. Exhale and release back to Mountain Pose, bringing palms of hands together. Breathe freely, tuning in once again to the brightness in the heart-space.

RESOURCES

Books

Concise Practice Guides

Adyashanti. *The Way of Liberation: A Practical Guide to Spiritual Enlightenment*. Campbell, CA: Open Gate Sangha, 2013.

Bhikkhu, Ajahn Sumano. *The Brightened Mind: A Simple Guide to Buddhist Meditation*. Wheaton, IL: Quest Books, 2011.

Gunaratana, Bhante. *Mindfulness in Plain English, 20th Anniversary Edition*. Somerville, MA: Wisdom Publications, 2011.

Loori, John Daido. *Finding the Still Point: A Beginner's Guide to Zen Meditation*. Boston, MA: Shambhala Publications, 2007.

McDonald, Kathleen. *How to Meditate: A Practical Guide*. Somerville, MA: Wisdom Publications, 2005.

Nhat Hanh, Thich. *How to Sit*. Berkeley, CA: Parallax Press, 2014.

Nhat Hanh, Thich. *The Long Road Turns to Joy: A Guide to Walking Meditation*. Berkeley, CA: Parallax Press, 2011.

Odier, Daniel. *The Doors of Joy: 19 Meditations for Authentic Living*. London, UK: Watkins Publishing, 2014.

Advaita Vedanta

Bennett, Francis. *I Am That I Am*. Salisbury, UK: Non-Duality Press, 2013.

Frawley, David. *Vedantic Meditation: Lighting the Flame of Awareness*. Berkeley, CA: North Atlantic Books, 2000.

Frazier, Jan. *The Freedom of Being: At Ease with What Is*. San Francisco, CA: Weiser Books, 2012.

Lucille, Francis. *Truth, Love & Beauty*. Temecula, CA: Truespeech Productions, 2006.

Wheeler, John. *You Were Never Born*. Salisbury, UK: Non-Duality Press, 2007.

The Ch'an & Zen Traditions

Fischer, Norman. *Training in Compassion: Zen Teachings on the Practice of Lojong*. Boston, MA: Shambhala Publications, 2013.

Nhat Hanh, Thich. *The Miracle of Mindfulness: An Introduction to the Practice of Meditation*. Boston, MA: Beacon Press, 1999.

Suzuki, Shunryu. *Zen Mind, Beginner's Mind: Informal Talks on Zen Meditation and Practice*. Boston, MA: Shambhala Publications, 2011.

Wei Wu Wei. *All Else Is Bondage: Non-Volitional Living*. Boulder, CO: Sentient Publications, 2004.

The Theravada Tradition

Goldstein, Joseph. *The Experience of Insight: A Simple and Direct Guide to Buddhist Meditation* (Shambhala Dragon Editions). Boston, MA: Shambhala Publications, 1987.

Kornfield, Jack. *Meditation for Beginners*. Boulder, CO: Sounds True, 2008.

Salzberg, Sharon. *Loving-Kindness: The Revolutionary Art of Happiness*. Boston, MA: Shambhala Publications, 2002.

The Tibetan Tradition

Chödrön, Pema. *How to Meditate: A Practical Guide to Making Friends with Your Mind*. Boulder, CO: Sounds True, 2013.

Kongtrul, Dzigar. *It's Up to You: The Practice of Self-Reflection on the Buddhist Path*. Boston, MA: Shambhala Publications, 2006.

Mingyur Rinpoche, Yongey. *The Joy of Living: Unlocking the Secret and Science of Happiness*. New York, NY: Harmony Books, 2007.

Thubten, Anam. *The Magic of Awareness*. Boston, MA: Snow Lion, 2012.

Yeshe, Lama Thubten. *When The Chocolate Runs Out*. Somerville, MA: Wisdom Publications, 2011.

Others

Schiffmann, Erich. *Yoga: The Spirit and Practice of Moving into Stillness*. New York, NY: Pocket Books, 1996.

Tolle, Eckhart. *The Power of Now: A Guide to Spiritual Enlightenment*. Novato, CA: New World Library, 1999.

Viljoen, Edward. *The Power of Meditation: An Ancient Technique to Access Your Inner Power*. New York, NY: Penguin, 2013.

Online Libraries

The Teachings of Ajahn Chah

www.ajahnchah.org

Sri Chinmoy Library

www.srichinmoylibrary.com

Organizations/Teaching Centers

Insight Meditation Society, Barre, MA

www.dharma.org

Spirit Rock: An Insight Meditation Center, Woodacre, CA

www.spiritrock.org

Video Talks

Ajahn Jayasaro on Meditation

www.youtube.com/watch?v=IP_rmBNAa9c

Guided Meditation—Ajahn Amaro—Relaxation of the Body

www.youtube.com/watch?v=mtnv9HgWpDE

A Guided Meditation on the Body, Space, and Awareness with
Yongey Mingyur Rinpoche

www.youtube.com/watch?v=5GSeWdjyr1c

MEDITATION INDEX

CPSIA information can be obtained at www.ICGtesting.com
Printed in the USA
BVOW03s1212090415

395234BV00001B/50/P

9 781623 154974